LLYFRGELL BARADE
WREXHAM COUNTY BOROUGH LIBRARY SERVICE

TYNNWYD
OR STOC

D0358228

WITHDRAWN
FROM STOCK

CORNWALL MURDER FILES

FAMOUS CASES SOLVED AND UNSOLVED

PATRICIA GRAY

HALSGROVE

First published in Great Britain in 2010

Copyright © Patricia Gray 2010

All rights reserved. No part of this publication may be reproduced,
stored in a retrieval system, or transmitted in any form or by any
means without the prior permission of the copyright holder.

British Library Cataloguing-in-Publication Data
A CIP record for this title is available from the British Library

ISBN 978 0 85704 059 6

HALSGROVE
Halsgrove House,
Ryelands Industrial Estate,
Bagley Road, Wellington, Somerset TA21 9PZ
Tel: 01823 653777   Fax: 01823 216796
email: sales@halsgrove.com

Part of the Halsgrove group of companies
Information on all Halsgrove titles is available at: www.halsgrove.com

Printed and bound by Short Run Press Ltd., Exeter

Contents

WREXHAM C.B.C LIBRARY	
LLYFRGELL B.S. WRECSAM	
C56 0000 0587 769	
Askews & Holts	29-Jul-2014
364.152309	£8.99
ANF	WR

Preface

Crime-wise, Cornwall is the fourth safest place to live in England and Wales according to recent statistics. Perhaps this, and the popular view that the county is a quiet backwater endowed with beautiful scenery, makes crimes of violence even more newsworthy, seemingly even more disturbing in the public's view.

The truth is most murders are the result of domestic friction of one kind or another, the victim and the perpetrator usually being known to each other. Most of the cases appearing in this book, murders committed within the past hundred years, prove the point that 'the ultimate crime' is most often motivated by those age-old human vices: anger, greed, jealousy lust, etc.

Many of these cases have been chosen because they required more than usual intelligence in solving them and in bringing the murderer to trial and conviction. And of course up until 1969, when capital punishment was abolished for murder in Great Britain, those convicted faced the ultimate penalty, adding an horrific and dramatic end to all such cases.

The book ends with intrigue, reviewing half a dozen unsolved cases for which the murderer has yet to be brought to book.

CHAPTER 1

Constantine: The Invisible Man

Early in her reign, Her Majesty Queen Elizabeth II granted amnesty to all who had deserted from the Services during the First and Second World Wars. The amnesty came just at the right time for William Garfield Rowe.

William was born in 1899. His family, who were farming near Porthleven when William was conscripted into the Army in 1917, were pacifists and William had no wish to fight and kill. After a few days soldiering he returned to Cornwall and the family farm. The Military Police found him, arrested him and took him to a detention centre. William escaped and made his way home again. While his father, mother and brothers spent the day working on the farm, William remained in the house. He never went out of the house in daylight but when darkness came he would do his share of the work on the farm. He became a recluse. No-one outside the family knew he was at home. Anyone who enquired about him was told that he had been killed in action in 1917.

Despite the fact that during the Second World War the whole population was registered to receive a ration book, identity card, and clothing coupons, the authorities never learned of William's existence. The family produced the food they needed so William was able to survive without registering.

William's father died in 1949. The family moved across the county to an isolated farm in Constantine. Nanjarrow was one and a half miles

from a main road, approached only by a rough track. It was sufficiently remote to allow William to continue his life as the invisible
man. The farm was run by William's brother, Stanley, who was still
single, as, of course, was William. Another brother, Joel, with whom
William had never got on well, had married and lived nearby. When
Stanley died, William farmed by night while his mother farmed by
day. They struggled on until she died in 1956. The amnesty for desert-
ers enabled William, now in his mid-fifties, to openly take over the
running of Nanjarrow. There was no longer any need to hide.
William could go to market or the shops, but old habits die hard and
William was shy and happy with his own company. When he needed
help with the farm he was able to hire labourers but visitors were dis-
couraged. William shut up all the rooms in the five-bedroom farmhouse except one. He left all the furniture and possessions in place
and lived in a downstairs room.

In 1960, on an occasion when William was away from the farm for a
few hours, the house was broken into and £200 in cash was stolen
together with some of his mother's jewellery. No-one was charged
with the offence.

On 15 August 1963 a neighbour saw a dead body lying in a corner of
the Nanjarrow farm yard. He called the police. PC James and another
officer responded. The Cornwall County Pathologist, Dr
F D M Hocking, arrived and found William Rowe lying face down
with one arm outstretched. He had been stabbed five times in quick
succession while he was standing upright. One of the stab wounds
was in his heart, two in his liver, one in the right hand side of his neck
which was so deep it went to the spine and severed the main blood
vessels in the side of the neck, and there was a superficial cut on the
front of the neck. His head had been battered by a series of blows
with a blunt instrument causing six splits in the scalp. Both eyes had
been blackened. There were scrapes, abrasions and cuts on the face

caused by the body falling and being dragged across the yard. There were bloodstains leading to the farmhouse door, a pool of blood on the doorstep and blood splashes on the door framework. There were drag marks in the mud between the door and the dead man. The house had been ransacked, with cupboards thrown open, drawers pulled out, furniture overturned and clothing strewn around.

The next day a Russell Pascoe was riding his motor-cycle in Constantine. Road blocks had been set up around the crime scene and Detective Sergeant Arscott recognised Pascoe as a man about whom the police had had suspicions for a long time. He asked Pascoe to go to the murder headquarters, which had been set up in a nearby school, for routine questioning. Detective Superintendent Maurice Osborne had been seconded from Scotland Yard to assist the Cornish police with the inquiry at the request of the Chief Constable of Cornwall. He spoke with Pascoe who said that he had read about the murder in the paper. When asked if he knew the farmer, Pascoe replied that he did and had worked for him three or four years ago. When asked to account for his movements the previous evening, he said he was at the caravan, where he had been living, with three girls and Dennis Whitty. Pascoe was a casual labourer who had left his wife, who was expecting another child in the New Year, and his 4 year old son and moved into a two-bed caravan at the Kenwyn Hill Caravan Park just outside Truro with Dennis John Whitty and three 19 year old girls. Whitty, who was a year younger than Pascoe, also worked as a casual labourer. In the caravan Whitty shared a bed with Bridget Hamilton, to whom he became engaged at Falmouth Police Station, while Pascoe shared a bed with Norma Teresa Booker and Margaret Ann Sweeny.

The police called Whitty in for questioning. Pascoe was asked to attend Falmouth Police Station on 17 August. Detective Superintendent Osborne told him the police had "good reason" to believe he and Whitty had killed Mr Rowe. Under caution Pascoe gave a statement in which he admitted knocking Rowe over the head with a bar. "I told Dennis that this was enough but he went mad with a knife. Last Wednesday night with my mate, Dennis Whitty, I went to Mr Rowe's farm. We went on my motor-cycle. We were going to see if he had any money. We knocked at the door at about 11 o'clock. The old man answered the door. Dennis was standing in front of the door. He said he was a helicopter pilot and had crashed. I hit the old man on the back of the head with a small iron bar. I had to walk away, honest I did. I went inside and found £4 under the piano. Dennis took a watch, two big boxes of matches and some keys from the old man's pockets. We shared the £4; £2 each. I have spent mine." Pascoe denied killing William Rowe. Whitty, he said, went mad. "I had to walk away. I couldn't stop him. He said he finished him when he stuck a knife in his throat. I only knocked him over the head with a bar. I just knocked him out. When I did I told Dennis that was enough but he went mad with the knife. Then he took the bar from me and kept thumping him on the head." When the police told Whitty that Pascoe had admitted they were both responsible, Whitty was adamant that "Pascoe made me stick him". They each blamed the other and continued to do so. When charged and cautioned, Whitty, said, "We are both over twenty-one so I suppose we can hang".

When Whitty realised the serious position he was in he made a confession under caution saying that Pascoe suggested they went to Nanjarrow for money. He said he didn't want to go but Pascoe made him. "I knocked and the old man came to the door with a lantern. I told him I'd had trouble with a helicopter and asked the old man to show me the phone." Whitty was wearing dark jeans and a double-breasted dark blazer with silver buttons which he hoped would be taken for naval uniform in the lantern light. Whitty said Pascoe, who had been against the wall, hit William Rowe on the head with an iron bar. The old man fell down and Pascoe continued hitting him while, at the same time, telling Whitty to "stick him". "I didn't want to and I started crying. He told me he would use the bar on me if I didn't do it, so I stuck him in the chest about three or four times and once in the throat, I think." Pascoe then made him drag the body to a corner of the yard and take some keys from the old man's pocket. They went into the house and took two packets of matches and an old watch. He had no idea what Pascoe did with the keys but he threw the knife away and dropped the bar in the dam.

In his statement, Pascoe said that on their way back to the caravan they threw the bar and the knife in the Argel Dam reservoir. The police recovered both weapons; an iron jemmy about fourteen inches long, weighing about 2lb 5oz, and a sheath knife six inches long, sharpened on both sides and tapering to a point. The police found the boxes of matches in the caravan. A fellow worker found the missing Elgin watch in the workmen's locker room at the Truro Gas Works in the pocket of a waterproof mackintosh which he knew Whitty had been wearing.

Russell Pascoe, a labourer, aged 23, married, and a native of Constantine, and Dennis Whitty, a labourer, aged 22, single, of St Keverne, Cornwall, appeared at Penryn Magistrates' Court on 19 August 1963 charged with the murder, on 14 August, of William Garfield Rowe, aged 64, a farmer of Constantine. The men stood in the dock handcuffed to police officers. They were remanded in custody until 16 September when the Penryn magistrates held a preliminary hearing of the Crown's case against them. Twenty-four witnesses were called for the prosecution, among them the three girls with whom the men shared the caravan. Norma Teresa Booker told the court the two men asked for nylon stockings before they went out with a starting gun, knife and an iron bar. When they returned Whitty had blood on his face. The next day, she added, Whitty said they did the murder and Pascoe said if the girls did not keep their mouths shut they would end up the same way.

Those in court were shocked when the extent of William Rowe's injuries were revealed by the prosecutor, who spoke of "a savage and brutal attack". Part of one finger on the victim's right hand had been almost completely severed as he struggled to defend himself. The prosecutor concluded by describing the crime as premeditated in that they both agreed they were going out in furtherance of theft and were prepared to attack anyone they encountered. It was cold-blooded and ruthless murder committed for gain. Pascoe and Whitty were committed to Bodmin Assizes.

On 29 October 1963 at Bodmin Assizes before Mr Justice Thesiger, Whitty and Pascoe were tried for murder. Witnesses put the terrible details of the crime before the jury. Whitty said in evidence that it was Pascoe's idea to rob the farmer. He said Pascoe had admitted to him that he had broken into the farm before and got £300. "I told him I did not want to go. He said, 'You will have to go, if you do not I will scar you for life'." Whitty told the court that he had left his home in St Keverne because it was haunted. His mother gave evidence that she agreed the house was haunted but admitted Whitty's father did not think so. The defence claimed Whitty suffered from mental hysteria.

It must have come as a shock to the killers when the prosecutor told the court that the intruders ransacked the farmhouse but missed finding £3,000; and that the police suspected thousands of pounds were hidden on the farm and in the buildings at Nanjarrow.

In his autobiography, Dr Hocking, the pathologist on the case, described Pascoe as "a simple lad, easily led" and Whitty as "a small fair-haired man who wore gold ear-rings and had a passion for eating snails". In his view, although shorter and younger, Whitty was almost a "little weasel of a man" and the dominant partner.

In his final address to the jury, Whitty's defence counsel, Mr Norman

Skelhorn, QC, submitted that Whitty was forced to do what he did under threats from Pascoe and asked the jury to say Whitty suffered from mental hysteria and could claim diminished responsibility. He asked the jury to acquit Whitty on the murder charge and bring in a verdict against him of manslaughter. Mr J Comyn, QC, for Pascoe urged the jury to find him not guilty of murder. They should accept his evidence as truthful whatever they thought of his character.

Summing up, the judge, Mr Justice Thesiger, cautioned the jury to be careful in accepting the evidence of either Whitty or Pascoe when each sought to blame the other. The jury took four and a quarter hours to bring in verdicts of "Guilty" of murder against both defendants.

Appeals against the sentences were heard and dismissed. Whitty was executed at Winchester Prison and Pascoe executed at Horfield Prison, Bristol, on 17 December 1963. The Bishop of Bristol, Dr Tomkins, issued a statement saying Pascoe had been baptised and confirmed beforehand.

Campaigners in Falmouth hoping to use the scheduled executions to build support for a petition to abolish capital punishment, had to abandon the petition for lack of support.

During their search of the farmhouse for evidence, the police found that Mr Rowe had hidden money about the property. They found too that he had spent the years when he had been hiding from the authorities in self-education. They found a tattered two-page document written in Spanish by William Rowe recording the places and amounts that he had hidden in the house, fields, pig-house floor, and hedges. Milk bottles stuffed with currency had the tops sealed with tallow and were inverted in a bucket topped with tallow. The money found belonged to relatives who have not revealed how much they

inherited. William Rowe's brother took over the running of Nanjarrow and had to discourage treasure-seekers by putting up barbed wire
barricades with a notice saying "Keep Out".

CHAPTER 2

Falmouth: A Quick Cop

It was a clever piece of detective work that led to a murderer being caught within twelve hours of his crime. Before the murderer realised he was under suspicion, and before he could destroy evidence, the police had their man.

Albert Bateman had been an accountant all his working life until he retired and took over Gooche's tobacconist shop in Commercial Chambers, Arwenack Street, Falmouth. The shop was near the docks and harbour and did a steady trade. Mr Bateman was an orderly man with a fixed routine. He closed the shop at 5.45pm or 5.50pm so that he could walk home and be in time for the 6pm radio *News*. He was so meticulous that if he was given a bank note that was torn, he would repair it with a paper strip before returning it to circulation.

On Christmas Eve 1942 there was a slight variation in Mr Bateman's routine. As the shop was busy, his wife brought him sandwiches for lunch which he ate in the shop. When he had not arrived home in time for the 6 o'clock *News* his wife assumed that a rush of last minute shoppers had delayed him. By 7.30pm Mrs Bateman was so anxious that she went to the shop to see if her husband was still there. Finding the shop locked and in darkness she returned home by another route in case her husband had varied his walk and been taken ill. Not finding him at the house she picked up a duplicate set of keys and hurried back to the shop. Finding it still in darkness she felt nervous of going in by herself and was relieved to see two policemen, Sergeant

Bennet and Police-Cadet Chinn, walking along Arwenack Street. Sergeant Bennet unlocked the shop and entered. The black-out curtains had not been pulled so he used his torch to look around the shop. At first nothing appeared to be out of place until Mr Bateman was discovered on the floor behind the counter with his head lying in a pool of blood. He was fully dressed and wearing his overcoat. It appeared Mr Bateman was on the point of closing the shop when he was attacked. Dr Harris was called; and he estimated Mr Bateman had been dead for two hours.

On the shop counter was a revolver and a blood-stained handkerchief. Mrs Bateman recognised the handkerchief as belonging to her husband. It was found that Mr Bateman had used his handkerchief to mop up the blood which welled from the initial blow to his chin.

Mrs Phyllis Cooper was an assistant at a tailor and outfitter's shop close to Mr Bateman's shop. She said that it was Mr Bateman's habit to end his day of business by picking up the mat outside the entrance to his shop, taking it inside, putting it in a cupboard under the stairs and banging the door shut. Then he would put on his overcoat, change his cap for his trilby and leave for home. She had heard him follow this routine on Christmas Eve.

Superintendent Thomas Morcumbe, Head of Falmouth Police, was sent for and he and the Cornwall County Pathologist, Dr F D M Hocking, examined the body before it was taken to the mortuary for the post-mortem.

A heavy blow had been struck to the chin, splitting the skin. There was a fracture of the skull and brain damage, which could have been the result of the victim falling backwards onto the floor. A further heavy blow had been struck to the face as he lay on the floor. Mr Bateman's top and bottom dentures had been smashed to pieces in the vicious attack and although some bits were found in the pool of blood on the floor by his head, others were found embedded in the blood clots in the back of the mouth. Blood in quantity had run down the air passages into the lungs and the air passages had become completely blocked. Mr Bateman had suffocated to death in his own blood as a direct result of the assault. The time of death was established as about 6pm the same day.

The shop premises looked undisturbed and there was no sign of a fight. £14 in notes was found on the body and £15.9s.4d in silver and coin was in an attaché case on a shelf. Mrs Bateman told the police that at least £25 was missing. The police read the crime scene as having an assailant who had waited until Mr Bateman had gone into the back of the shop with the door mat and then dashed in, grabbed cash from the till and been confronted by the tobacconist before he could make his escape.

The revolver found on the counter was not loaded nor had it been fired recently. Mrs Bateman said it had not belonged to her husband. The police realised that the weapon had been intended to hold-up and frighten the victim. While Mr Bateman was at the back of the shop, the thief entered, put the revolver down on the counter when he reached out to steal from the till and overlooked it in his panic to get away after assaulting the shopkeeper. No fingerprints were found on the Webley service revolver but its number, 33748, was immediately recognised by Superintendent Morcumb.

In the February of 1942 that particular revolver had been reported missing from a load of arms moved by crane in Falmouth dock. Among the dozen or so people interviewed about the theft was Gordon Horace Trenoweth, a 33 year old stevedore, who had unloaded the jib crane. He had had the opportunity to take the gun and the police found that he had a conviction for larceny in his younger days. He had agreed to the police searching his home but no gun was found.

Eleven hours after the murder, at 3.45am on Christmas morning, Superintendent Morcumb and Inspector Martin called at Mallin's Cottage, Falmouth, the home of Gordon Trenoweth and found him in bed. Beside the bed was a suit of clothes and a pair of brown shoes. Blood stains were visible on the right sleeve of the jacket and tiny specks of blood on the shoes.

Gordon Trenoweth was taken to the Police Station and asked to say how he had spent the previous afternoon and evening. He said he had spent the afternoon shopping and walking around the town. He had caught the 7pm bus to Truro and spent the evening with friends. Two packets of Woodbine cigarettes had been found on him together with £5.9s.9d. Offered a Players cigarette he said he preferred Wood- bines. When told that a man had been found with severe facial injuries, Trenoweth made a reply the police found significant: "I bought the cigarettes at Pearce's. I was not in that man's shop". He refused to account for the money found on him. He explained the blood on his clothing and shoes by saying he had had a nose bleed.

Dr Hocking examined the detained man and found there was no sign of any recent nose-bleed. He found traces of blood on a hand and at the side of a nail. At 10 pm on Christmas Day Superintendent Mor- cumbe charged Gordon Trenoweth with the murder.

His clothes and the Webley revolver were passed to Dr Hocking for forensic examination. Dr Hocking reported that the suit was of good quality and not much worn and that the right cuff of a shirt Trenoweth had been wearing showed traces of human blood. An unsuccessful attempt had been made to wash the stains away. Human bloodstains were found on the accused man's waistcoat and jacket. The bottom of the left hand trouser pocket had a one and a half to two inch tear which was not due to wear but had been made deliberately to allow the revolver to be carried concealed. The oil on the revolver caused bits of fluff found in the left-hand pocket of the trousers to adhere to it. Fibres had also stuck to the gun which were found to have come from a strip of carpet in the junk-filled loft at Mallin's Cottage where the gun had probably been hidden.

When the £1 notes found in Trenoweth's clothes were examined, one was found to have had a tear at one corner which had been repaired with a piece of white paper. The police returned to Mr Bateman's shop and searched through all the waste paper. They found a crumpled bill-head with a corner sharply cut out that was an exact fit with the piece used to repair the note found on Gordon Trenoweth. They sent the bill-head, the £1 note and the gum Mr Bateman used to mend notes to the Forensic Laboratory in Bristol. Their report confirmed that the piece cut out of the bill-head exactly matched that used to repair the £1 note. The gum in the shop and that used to repair the note were identical. The police also found a witness who, on Christmas Eve, had seen Mr Bateman repairing a note. The police were also able to establish that the Woodbines found on Trenoweth had been delivered to Mr Bateman's shop and not to Pearce's.

On 11 February 1943 Gordon Horace Trenoweth appeared before Mr Justice Tucker at Exeter Assizes charged with the murder of 61 year old Albert Bateman. He pleaded "Not Guilty".

After the prosecutor, Mr J D Casswell, KC, had outlined the case for the Crown, Mrs Bateman gave evidence. At the end of her examination she collapsed and had to be carried from the court. Reginald John Pearce told the court that the accused had not bought cigarettes in his shop.

Dorothy Allen of Truro gave evidence about having a drink with

Trenoweth at The Market Inn, Truro, on 23 December and arranging to meet him again on Christmas Eve. He arrived late for that date saying he had been working and had to have a wash and change of clothes, and as a result he had missed the 6.15pm bus to Truro and had to catch the 7 o'clock bus. He told her he had plenty of money and paid for drinks for her, two for her mother, and one each for two soldiers. Before he left he said he would buy her a pair of shoes. She said she would rather have the money and he gave her a £1 note. Cross-examined, she said Trenoweth had previously given her cigarettes and money but never as much as a pound. The barman at The Market Inn confirmed he had served Trenoweth with drinks on Christmas Eve and taken money from him to pay for drinks for other people.

Witnesses were called to give evidence that Mr Bateman had been seen just before 6pm in his shop and that the accused was in the vicinity at different times. Experts gave evidence that the blood found on Trenoweth was not of his blood group but was of Mr Bateman's blood group.

Superintendent Morcumb told the jury that Trenoweth had said to him that he (Trenoweth) had had only three or four pounds on him when he caught the bus to Truro. Asked to explain how he had £5.9s.9d on him when arrested, Trenoweth had said, "I don't want to say anything more about the money".

Mr J Scott Henderson, KC, for the defence called members of Trenoweth's family to testify that he had been at home at the time of the murder.

Gordon Trenoweth went into the witness box and told the court that in January 1941 his wife had been taken into a mental home. When he had visited her he found she was working in the home. Feeling strongly that it was wrong he should be expected to pay maintenance for her when she was working, he refused to pay and was sent to prison. He came out of prison in November 1942 and in the next few weeks earned, or had in his possession, £18.5s.3d of which he gave his mother 30 shillings a week. He said he had spent Christmas Eve trying to find a job, shopping, walking around, buying a pasty at midday instead of going home, and punctuating the day with visits to pubs. He said that when Superintendent Morcumb questioned him on Christmas Day he assumed it was in connection with his failure to pay maintenance for his wife.

Summing up for the defence, Mr Scott Henderson tried to show the accused man was not at Mr Bateman's shop at the crucial time. Mr Casswell, for the prosecution, pointed out that the bloodstains, the repaired £1 note, and the fragments of material from the accused's trouser pocket found on the revolver, were strong elements of proof that he had committed the crime.

In his summing up the judge pointed out to the jury that there were no fingerprints on the gun and no blood on the accused's shoes. If the evidence of the prisoner's family was correct he could not have been near the dead man's shop at the time of the crime.

The jury took two hours to deliver a unanimous verdict of "Guilty" with a strong recommendation for mercy as it was considered the accused had not meant to kill.

The trial, which had lasted five days, culminated in the judge putting on the black cap and pronouncing the sentence of death. On 22 March 1943 the Court of Criminal Appeal dismissed Trenoweth's appeal. The recommendation for mercy did not lead to a reprieve.

CHAPTER 3

Isles of Scilly: Cruelty

Wolliam Thomas Menheniott, always known as "Tom", was born in Cornwall in 1924. When he was three months old his mother died. As his father was blind, Tom and his older brother, three year old George, were taken into care in May 1924 and brought up in a Children's Home in Cornwall. The regime in the Home was harsh and enforced with corporal punishment, which was not good training for future parenting.

When he was 14 George ran away and found work on a farm, then joined the Army as soon as he was old enough. In his turn, Tom too ran away and joined the Army in which he learned the trade of a motor mechanic. Tom married in the 1940s and in 1948 had a daughter. He received a prison sentence for neglecting the child. A boy born in 1949 was taken into care and remained in care until he died at 17. Tom left his wife in about 1950 and went to live with Elizabeth Thomas, who took the name Menheniott although they never married.

Together they had six children, the last of whom died in infancy. A boy born in 1950 and a girl born in 1952 were taken into care by Cornwall County Council in 1953 when both Tom and Elizabeth were given prison sentences for neglect of the children. When they were released they went to Kent where a second son was born in 1955. He was taken into care when the family became homeless. A second daughter was born in 1956 and their fifth child, Stephen Richard, was born in Redhill County Hospital on 4 June 1957. His parents were living in a caravan but became homeless so Stephen and his sister were taken into care. At the end of January 1958 their daughter was returned to them but Stephen was in poor health and not allowed home until August. His parents moved to Hailsham in East Sussex and four months later Stephen was admitted to hospital in an under-nourished condition. An NSPCC Inspector described the conditions in which the Menheniotts lived as "deplorable". While in hospital Stephen was taken into care by East Sussex County Council and placed in a residential nursery. The Council assumed parental rights over him until the age of 18 or until the resolution was rescinded.

In 1965 Tom got a job in Cornwall with a daffodil farmer on the Isles of Scilly. The job came with a cottage so Tom and Elizabeth moved to Holy Vale on the main island of St Mary's. Holy Vale is an isolated hamlet on the far side of St Mary's comprising a farm and a row of three cottages, of which one was empty and one a holiday home at that time. Tom was not popular but he was seen as "a local character". A powerfully built man, he was known for his bad temper and bad language but he was capable of kindness and was considered useful because of his skills with mechanical things which he sometimes prac-tised without charge. He got on well with his employer and was good at his job. He had given up heavy drinking but his children were afraid of him.

In 1969 Tom's younger daughter, who was 13, became pregnant and Tom was charged with incest and acquitted. The daughter was taken into care by the Isles of Scilly Council. The islanders felt Tom had been wrongly acquitted and relations deteriorated. Elizabeth Thomas moved to the mainland.

From time to time the children were released from care and went to live with him. During 1971 and 1972 Stephen was allowed to visit his family at Holy Vale. In 1972, when he was 15, Stephen left school; East Sussex Social Services were unable to find him a job or a place to live. The boy wanted to go home, so the decision was taken to discharge him into his father's care and supervision passed to Cornwall County Council Social Services Department. The Cornish department told East Sussex Social Services that Stephen should not be sent home and that they would not accept responsibility for him. East Sussex ignored advice from the Childrens' Officer that Thomas Menheniott was a dangerous man with an uncontrollable temper who would not be able to cope with the boy. East Sussex sent him home and washed their hands of him. The Isles of Scilly Social Services Department said they would see what they could do in the difficult circumstances. In the event none of the departments monitored Stephen's progress.

Stephen got a job in the Co-op supermarket on St Mary's but was dismissed after six months for poor hygiene; and worked for a farmer but was not up to the job. So he stayed at home and did the housework as well as fieldwork. His sister Elizabeth, always called "Liz", had a common-law relationship and took the surname Rayner. She lived at Holy Vale with her two small sons and it was Stephen's job to look after them, change their nappies and feed them. Stephen was treated as a lackey and subjected to much abuse.

When he was not working Stephen claimed unemployment benefit but the staff at the Social Security Office failed to see signs that Stephen was being abused at home. Stephen himself never complained to anyone about the way he was treated although some thought he was treated worse than a dog. Thomas Menheniott was a man who did not suffer fools gladly and he was unable to understand the needs of his backward son. Stephen's slowness and dull wits exacerbated his father's quick temper.

One of the few people on St Mary's who expressed any concern about the boy was the island dentist, Mr Fairest, who had to treat Stephen when the boy's front teeth were broken down to the gums. He made a denture to remedy the damage but did not believe the story he was told, that the teeth had been broken by Stephen falling out of a tree. He observed that Stephen was afraid of his father. Mr Fairest's professional ethics restricted what he could do but he discussed the case with the Specialist in Community Medicine whose job it was to investigate non-accidental injuries to children.

Stephen disappeared in 1976. In December that year the police began enquiries into Stephen's whereabouts. Tom told them Stephen had gone back to the mainland and was staying at the home of a girl friend in Hove and at their request gave them the girl's name and address. When the police traced the girl she said she had been friendly with Stephen but had not seen him for two years. Tom produced a letter to the police, which he had forged, purportedly from Stephen saying he would not be returning to the island. Elizabeth Rayner, who had shared the home with Tom and Stephen, was questioned. Her conscience appears to have been bothering her and the stress of keeping a secret undermined her health. She confessed to the police that her father had been having sex with her since she was 15 and told them that Stephen was dead and had been buried on the farm. She showed the police where the shallow grave had been dug in the corner of California field. The police cleared the brambles, the carefully placed logs, and the bulbs she had planted on the grave before they dug the swampy ground and uncovered the body. It was badly decomposed and had to be identified by Mr Fairest, the dentist.

A post-mortem was carried out by Dr Hunt, the Home Office Pathologist, on 18 May 1977. The lack of soft tissue and organs hampered establishing the cause of death. Dr Hunt found that the skeleton had fractures at the back of the 5th, 6th and 7th ribs caused two or three months before death and only recently healed. Dr Hunt was sure they had caused the boy much pain. The 7th rib had been re-broken not long before death. At the Coroner's Inquest Dr Hunt told the jury that no cause of death could be established with any certainty because of the advanced decomposition.

The police had arrested Thomas Menheniott on suspicion of murder in May 1976. In July he was charged with the murder of his son and incest with his daughter, Elizabeth Rayner. At the Committal Proceedings on 17 August 1977 in respect of the murder, no evidence was offered on the charge of incest and it did not proceed.

At Bodmin Crown Court on Tuesday 6 December 1977, before Mr Justice Willis, Thomas Menheniott, 53, stood trial for the murder of his 18 year-old son. He also faced four charges of causing grievous bodily harm and a charge of preventing the holding of an inquest by burying the body. He pleaded "Guilty" to the last charge and "Not Guilty" to the other five. Mr David Owen-Thomas, QC, appeared for the Crown and Mr T G Field-Fisher, QC, for the defence.

Mr Owen-Thomas opened by telling the Court that the Menheniott family home was described as being sordid, untidy, unkempt, inadequately furnished but clean. He said they would hear that Thomas Menheniott treated Stephen like a lackey, beating him savagely with high tension cables, a shovel, a fence post and a potato tray. Stephen had a scaffolding pole slammed into his back, a knife thrown at him, tea poured over him and was punched repeatedly. He produced Stephen's skull and ribs to show how they had been broken; and said the shovel which had hit Stephen on the back could have caused the ribs to break; and the scaffolding pole slammed into his back could have re-broken the 7th rib. Stephen was tethered outside his cottage home and was not allowed to leave the farm for fear that people would see the tell-tale marks of violence.

Elizabeth Rayner was the chief witness. She had had a stroke earlier in the year and moved very slowly. She said her brother was dull-witted and subnormal and that she thought her father was not wholly normal in his outbursts of violence against the boy. She said her father and Stephen were always rowing. Around Christmas 1975 she had intervened in a quarrel between her father and Stephen who were having a verbal fight in the downstairs passage. After her intervention her father went upstairs to his bedroom to watch television while Stephen went to the bathroom on the ground floor and she helped him to have a bath. After his bath he went upstairs to his father's bedroom to have his legs dressed.

Stephen suffered, as many other islanders did, from "flower rash" caused by sensitivity to daffodils. His father always dressed and bandaged Stephen's legs for him. This small act of care was confirmed at the post-mortem when bandages were found around the lower legs of the skeleton. It was usual for Stephen to hold on to the door and put one foot on his father's bed to enable his father to treat his leg. He then would put the other foot on the bed for the other leg to be dressed. On this occasion Stephen was not standing still, which irritated his father who yanked Stephen around. Stephen hit his head on the wall, fell to the floor and did not get up. He crawled into his own bedroom where he lay groaning. When Elizabeth found Stephen on the floor she called their father and together they lifted Stephen onto his bed. She said Stephen was semi-conscious, dazed and mumbling. She said she kept going in about every half an hour to check on him.

At first he was able to answer when she spoke to him but later in the night he became unconscious. He was cold so Elizabeth Rayner said she fetched a hot water bottle for him and she or her father continued to check on him every half an hour. Stephen was breathing and moaning. The moaning annoyed her father who yelled repeatedly at Stephen to no avail. Mrs Rayner added to her earlier evidence by saying that during the row in the passage her father had given Stephen "rabbit punches". When Thomas Menheniott went into Stephen's room at 3am Stephen was dead. Her father was unwilling to call a doctor because the bruises and injuries on Stephen's body would be discovered. Mrs Rayner was reluctant to answer questions about the nature of the injuries but she did say there was a mark low down on Stephen's back. It was decided to bury the body on the farm and the next day a place was found where the ground was soft enough for a shallow grave to be dug. Elizabeth Rayner and her father placed the body in the car and drove near to California field, put the body into a wheelbarrow, covered it with tarpaulin and took it to the waiting grave. Her father gave out that Stephen had returned to East Sussex to work.

Dr Hunt explained to the jury the finding of Stephen's body and how the grave had been searched for missing teeth but none were found. He said the ribs were partially mended when the 7th rib was re-broken just before death. It was possible the rib had pierced the lung membrane leading to death. Stephen's fall in his father's bedroom could have caused concussion, with fatal results. At the time of his death Stephen had been thin and malnourished.

Mr Fairest testified that four of Stephen's teeth had been broken back to the gum line. Where two more teeth were missing from the skull it could be seen that the gum had not healed, proving that the teeth must have been knocked out just before death. As no teeth were found in the grave they could not have been knocked out when stones and earth were thrown on the body.

Margaret Allwright, Stephen's elder sister by one year, gave evidence that she had frequently seen Stephen knocked about but not badly enough for her to make a complaint to any authority. She said her father mostly used his fists on the boy and when he fell would kick him ("put the boot in") before walking off and leaving Stephen in agony on the floor. Her husband, Adrian Allwright, told of how Stephen was treated as a slave by his father. Stephen's oldest brother, William, told the Court of the events which led him to believe Stephen was treated as a lackey. William's wife, Heather, gave evidence of the bruises and broken teeth she saw on Stephen on Boxing Day 1975.

John Russell Banfield, the farmer who lived in Holy Vale farm, testified how he had seen Stephen tethered by a long rope to the greenhouse. Another witness told of seeing Stephen being beaten with a piece of wood.

The defence case was that Stephen's death was the accidental result of falling while his legs were being dressed. Dr F D M Hocking, the former Cornwall County Pathologist, was called to testify that a blow to the head does not necessarily result in a fracture or serious internal bleeding but can cause concussion and various degrees of unconsciousness. Dr Hocking explained the ways in which death can occur if this state is neglected. The restless boy could have turned over and buried his face in his bedclothes and suffocated. Suffocation through the inhalation of vomit often happened or suffocation due to the patient lying on his back and his tongue falling backwards and obstructing the air entry to the lungs. To the suggestion that when the 7th rib was re-broken it punctured the lungs causing death, Dr Hocking said that Stephen's symptoms were not consistent with that theory. It is not easy for a bone to puncture a lung, as great force would be required, such as might happen in a motor accident.

Dr Hunt was recalled for cross-examination by the defence counsel. Mr Field-Fisher put to him Dr Hocking's suggestion that death was due to suffocation. Dr Hunt agreed he could not rule out the possibility. Professor Keith Mant of the Forensic Pathology Department of

Guy's Hospital told the Court that he agreed with the findings of both Dr Hunt and Dr Hocking but he preferred Dr Hocking's finding that Stephen died as a result of the blow to the head.

In his summing up for the jury, Mr Justice Willis stressed that much depended on whether Elizabeth Rayner's evidence could be relied upon. Margaret Allwright disliked her father so much that little reliance could be placed on her evidence.

On the ninth day of the trial the jury of two women and ten men took almost four hours to reach a majority verdict of "Guilty" to murder. Eleven jurors were for a "Guilty" verdict and one against. They were discharged from returning a verdict on the four charges of causing grievous bodily harm. Mr Justice Willis sentenced Menheniott to life imprisonment for the murder and five years' imprisonment for the offence of preventing an inquest, to run concurrently.

When Menheniott had been taken from the court, Mr Justice Willis expressed his concern that no-one on St Mary's, "with the honourable exception of the dentist", had done anything to help Stephen, who was obviously afraid of his father. He said that from time to time the boy must have shown signs of the painful injuries of one type or another. He thought it must have been obvious to everyone on St Mary's that the boy was being ill-treated. Mr Justice Wills called for a government inquiry into the shortcomings of the East Sussex Social Services Department in allowing Stephen to live with his father without supervision and wrote to the Secretary of State for Social Justice, Mr David Ennals, asking him to inquire into the case of Stephen Menheniott.

On 20 December 1977 an internal inquiry by East Sussex County Council found that the Council failed to properly supervise Stephen once he had gone to live with his father.

Mr David Ennals, Secretary of State for Social Justice, instituted a departmental inquiry by an outside team of three people in January 1978, which reported in September 1978. The Inquiry Team met Elizabeth Menheniott, her other children, and Stephen's uncle, George Menheniott, then a chauffeur and gardener living in Hampshire, as well as members of Cornwall and East Sussex County Councils and the Council of the Isles of Scilly, employees of the health authorities involved, and officers of the Devon and Cornwall Constabulary. The inquiry found that:

- too great an emphasis was placed on Stephen's wishes to return to his family and too little on the opinion of officials who had knowledge of Stephen and his family;

- East Sussex County Council's decision not to confer with Cornwall County Council on the case and to close the case on Stephen before his eighteenth birthday was indefensible;

- the withdrawal of Cornwall County Council from the case was justifiable on both professional and statutory grounds;

- the arrangement between East Sussex County Council and the Council of the Isles of Scilly for the latter to keep an eye on Stephen was too informal and ineffective;

- the problems were exacerbated by the Menheniott children having been in the care of several different authorities; and

- major reorganisations were taking place in Social Services departments at the time and staff were under great pressure.

CHAPTER 4

Lewannick: Blue Sandwiches

There was nationwide interest in the hunt for Sarah Ann Hearn, always known as "Annie", and in her subsequent trial at Bodmin Assizes in June 1931.

Mrs Hearn described herself as a widow who had married a medical student, Leonard Wilmot Hearn, in a register office "near Bedford Square", London, in 1919. They lived together for only a week after which they parted. She said that a day or two later she read in a Harrogate newspaper that he had died. When Mrs Hearn herself became news, a search was made of the national registry held at Somerset House but no marriage entry could be found for her, nor could the register office of which she had spoken be identified. When, during her trial, the judge asked her about her "marriage lines", or certificate, she had no idea what he was talking about. She gave her relatives a photograph of her late "husband", a handsome man. Years later, when she was in the spotlight, it was found that the photograph was a likeness of Lieutenant Charles Stewart Vane-Tempest, a grandson of the third Marquess of Londonderry. Mrs Hearn must have bought the photo. The young soldier had been killed in action in 1917. None of this was relevant to the charge she faced but it did throw doubt on her relationship with the truth.

Mrs Hearn lived for a time in Harrogate helping an aunt to run a cookery school. In about 1917 she looked after her two sisters, Mabel and Lydia, known as "Minnie". After Mabel died, Minnie went to live with Mrs Hearn in Harrogate. They moved to Cornwall in 1921 in the hope that Minnie's health would improve in the softer climate. In 1925 Mrs Hearn and Minnie moved to Trenhorne House to look after an aunt. Minnie, who had suffered ill-health all her life, was weak with so many complaints at the time of the move that the doctor himself transported her to their new home in his car. Trenhorne House was a semi-detached property in the small village of Lewannick, some six miles from Launceston.

When the aunt died in 1926 she left the property to Mrs Hearn and the sisters continued to live there. They had become friends with their nearest neighbours who lived at Trenhorne Farm. William and Alice Thomas were regular visitors and took the sisters on outings. William would often call bringing the newspaper and food treats prepared by his wife to tempt Minnie's appetite. The sisters lived in straitened circumstances and on one occasion, in 1928, Mr Thomas made Mrs Hearn a temporary loan of £38 to help them out. £38 was a lot of money in those days. Minnie's health did not improve. The doctor was a regular visitor because she had heart trouble, a life-long gastric illness and trouble with her eyes. He treated her for colitis but the stomach pains and vomiting persisted. She lost feeling in her hands and feet. When she died the doctor certified that her death had been caused by colitis and chronic gastric catarrh. Minnie was buried in Lewannick churchyard, as her aunt had been.

The Thomases felt sorry for Mrs Hearn. They kept up the friendship and invited her to join them on outings. Sometimes Mrs Thomas would prepare a picnic for them to take, sometimes Mrs Hearn prepared one, and sometimes they both made the picnic. On 18 October 1930 Mr and Mrs Thomas arranged to take Mr Thomas's mother, who had been staying with them, back to her own home in Bude. At midday, out of the blue, Mrs Thomas told her husband to invite Mrs Hearn to accompany them. Mrs Hearn opened a tin of salmon and made some sandwiches for a picnic. They left at 3pm and took Mrs Thomas Senior home. Mr Thomas went to get his hair cut while Mrs Thomas and Mrs Hearn walked around looking at the shops. At 5pm they met up at Littlejohns' Café where they ordered tea and cakes. Mrs Hearn produced the sandwiches wrapped in paper, put them on the table and unwrapped them for everyone to help themselves. There were six sandwiches in two piles of three. There was no handing around of the sandwiches; each person helped himself. After tea Mr Thomas went to the Globe Hotel where he had a shot of whisky to clear away the nausea he had felt after tea. When they met up again Mrs Thomas complained of having a "sweety" taste in her mouth and her husband bought her some bananas. On the drive home the car had to be stopped to allow Mrs Thomas to be sick; she was at the road-side vomiting for about half an hour. They continued the journey to Launceston where they parked the car and Mr Thomas left the women while he went to conduct some business. He returned at 7.30pm to find his wife had been sick again. They left Launceston and drove straight home. Mr Thomas, with Mrs Hearn's assistance, put his wife to bed; then went to call the doctor and to get some brandy for his wife. Dr Saunders examined Mrs Thomas and declared her to be suffering from food poisoning. According to the report in *The Times* he prescribed a diet of whitebait; kaolin, a refined form of china clay; and only water to drink. Mr Thomas and his wife asked Mrs Hearn to stay at the farm to look after Mrs Thomas and to cook for Mr Thomas and the live-in farm labourer, Mr Wilson. Mrs Hearn said she had not been feeling well at one stage.

Mrs Thomas's illness caused much local gossip. Mr Thomas asked Mrs Hearn what had been in the sandwiches because everyone was thinking they were the cause of the trouble. When the doctor called on 21 October he found the patient was slightly better. By 24 October Mrs Thomas had developed peripheral neuritis, a tingling of the feet and legs, in addition to the vomiting, diarrhoea and cramps which still persisted. On 29 October Mr Thomas drove over to get Mrs Thomas's mother, Mrs Tryphena Parsons, to cheer up his wife. Mrs Parsons moved in to nurse her daughter and to help Mrs Hearn with the cooking. Mrs Parsons, Mrs Hearn and Mr Thomas were all involved in giving Mrs Thomas her medication which included Genasprin, a form of aspirin. On 1 November the doctor said Mrs Thomas could have a fuller diet in order to replenish her strength. The next day Mrs Hearn cooked some mutton while Mrs Parsons prepared the gravy and served the meal. Mr Thomas carried his wife downstairs to eat but she found she had no appetite. Mrs Parsons expressed concern to Mr Thomas and he coaxed his wife into eating the meal. When Mrs Thomas was carried back to bed she was given three Genasprin. On 3 November Mr Thomas was awakened by his wife calling to him to take her into his room. She had been sharing a room with her mother. Mrs Thomas suffered a prolonged nosebleed and Dr Saunders called in a consultant from Plymouth, Dr Lister. He diagnosed arsenical poisoning and Mrs Thomas was taken to Plymouth City Hospital, where she died early next morning.

A post-mortem examination found no symptoms of natural disease but did find white arsenic which was in a form which could be obtained from weed killer. Mrs Hearn claimed that when Mr Thomas told her the results of the post-mortem he said some of Mrs Thomas's organs were being sent for analysis. He told her, "They will find out what it is and they will blame one of us. The blame will come heavier on you than me. People are saying so and a detective may be here at any time. Whatever there is they will find it out". Mrs Hearn, already distressed by the gossiping going on, must have felt very threatened. She said, "If people think like that I had better go to my own house".

On 6 November Mr Thomas asked Mrs Hearn for a written acknowledgement of the money he had lent her, having previously dismissed her offer of written acknowledgement. She complied immediately with his request.   Later she thought he was trying to distance himself from her.

Gossip was rife in Lewannick and the surrounding area. After Mrs Thomas' funeral her brother, Percy Parsons, made a point of asking Mrs Hearn if the sandwiches had been made at the farm. When Mrs Hearn replied "No", he said "This matter will have to be looked into".

On 10 November Mr Thomas received a letter from Mrs Hearn which said:

> *Dear Mr Thomas*
> *Goodbye. I am going out if I can. I cannot forget that awful man and the things he said. I am* innocent, innocent *but she is dead and it was my lunch she ate. I cannot stay. When I am gone they will be sure I am guilty, and you, at least, will be clear. May your dear wife's presence guard and comfort you still. Yours A.H.*

The word "gone" was written over the word "dead", which had been crossed out. There was a postscript to the note:

My life is not a great thing now dear Minnie has gone. I shall be glad if you will send my love to dear Bessie. Tell them not to worry about me. I shall be all right. My conscience is clear. I am not afraid of afterwards. I am giving instructions about selling the things and hope you will be paid in full. That is all I can do now.

Bessie was another of Mrs Hearn's sisters.

On receipt of the letter Mr Thomas took it straight to the police. They went to Trenhorne House and found no-one there. A search of the property found no arsenic in any form.   Mrs Hearn had disappeared but shortly afterwards her coat was found on the top of a cliff at Looe and one of her shoes washed up on the beach. Together with the note it looked as though Mrs Hearn had committed suicide; but the police were not convinced. Her disappearance at a critical moment was bound to throw suspicion on her conduct.

The inquest into the death of Alice Thomas opened on 24 November. Mr Thomas was questioned about his wife's illness and death. He agreed there were sheep dip and worming concoctions on the farm but denied there were any other poisons on the property. He told the Inquest his wife had never objected to his friendship with Mrs Hearn and he had given her no reason to be jealous. A member of the staff of a Launceston grocer and chemist shop gave evidence that in 1926 Mrs Hearn had bought a 1lb tin of arsenic-based weedkiller. Mrs Hearn's defence team would establish later that the arsenic-based weedkiller she had bought was blue in colour. There had been no other sales of any poisons or poisonous materials elsewhere in the surrounding area to Mrs Hearn, the Thomas or Parsons families. The Coroner's Inquest found that Mrs Thomas had died of arsenical poisoning.

The police obtained exhumation orders and the bodies of Minnie Everard and her aunt were taken from their graves. Traces of arsenic were found and the Coroner's Inquest returned a verdict of arsenical poisoning by a person or persons unknown.

The police issued and circulated a "Wanted" poster for Mrs Hearn, describing her as 5'3" tall, with brown hair, grey eyes, and a sallow complexion. She walked briskly, held her head slightly to the left, was well-spoken and had a reserved manner.

The *Daily Mail* published a photograph of Mrs Hearn and offered a reward of £500 to anyone who could confirm Mrs Hearn's death or give information that would enable the police to interview her.

Mr Cecil Powell, an architect living in Torquay, recognised his house-keeper as Mrs Hearn and contacted the police. It transpired that Mrs Hearn had left Trenhorne House; taken a taxi to Looe; and from there, travelled to Torquay, where she registered at St Leonard's Hotel as Mrs Ferguson of Heavitree, Exeter. She left the next day saying she was expecting her husband. That same afternoon she went to the house of a Mrs Marker who let lodgings. Calling herself Mrs Faithful, she said her husband was in Torquay Hospital.

On 12 November she answered an advertisement for a general servant placed in the local paper by Mr Powell. She wrote that her husband had died two years before. She had let rooms but could not make them pay; and the comfortable home advertised appealed to her. She enclosed an excellent reference for Mrs Faithful which was written from "The Larches, Heavitree, Exeter" and signed by "Dr and Mrs B Watson, late of Mannamead, Plymouth". Mr Powell employed her and was highly satisfied with her work. The police found that the address in Exeter given in the letter did not exist.

When Mrs Hearn was arrested in a street in Torquay she insisted her name was Mrs Dennis and continued to do so until confronted by Police Sergeant Trebilcock from Lewannick who recognised her.

Mrs Hearn was charged with the murder of Mrs Thomas and appeared at Launceston Magistrates' Court. She was further charged on 24 February with the murder of Minnie Everard. Mrs Elizabeth Spear, who shared the tenancy of Trenhorne House, told the Bench that Minnie was always in a delicate state and Mrs Hearn was a devoted sister who did all she could to nurse her. Mrs Spear said on two occasions Mrs Hearn had asked her to call the doctor. The magistrates heard the prosecution evidence and committed Mrs Hearn to Bodmin Assizes to stand trial on both charges.

Mr Powell received the £500 reward from the *Daily Mail* and handed it to Mr Walter West, an able solicitor of his acquaintance, to enable his housekeeper to have the best barrister in the land to defend her. Thus the brilliant Mr Norman Birkett, KC, later Lord Birkett, came to lead the defence team.

The trial opened before Mr Justice Roche at the Bodmin Assizes on 15 June 1931. There was such great hostility and prejudice against Mrs Hearn locally that it was necessary to empanel a jury drawn from the other side of the county. Mrs Hearn faced two separate charges; one in respect of Miss Everard and the other in respect of Mrs Thomas. When the charges were put to her, Mrs Hearn replied to each, "I am not guilty, Sir". The Crown decided to proceed first with the murder of Mrs Thomas. The prosecution was led by Mr H du Parcq, KC, later Lord du Parcq. In his opening statement to the jury, Mr du Parcq outlined the events of the trip to Bude and Mrs Thomas's illness. The prosecution alleged that Mrs Thomas was recovering when a second dose of arsenic was given to her sometime after 18 October but before her mother joined the household. Mr du Parcq mentioned the supposed suicide note and outlined Mrs Hearn's flight and discovery in Torquay. He called Mr Thomas who described the events leading up to his wife's death.

Cross-examined by Mr Birkett, Mr Thomas made it plain that the invitation to Mrs Hearn to join the trip to Bude was quite spontaneous and there was no juggling of the sandwiches. He admitted telling Mrs Hearn that people were gossiping about the two of them, and about the sandwiches for which, he told her, the blame would fall on her. Mr Birkett elicited more testimony to show Mrs Hearn as a distressed woman who was victim of the most horrible gossip.

Mr Percy Parsons, Mrs Thomas's brother, denied accusing Mrs Hearn of poisoning his sister at the funeral but admitted saying the matter should be looked into. Whatever Mr Parsons did say to Mrs Hearn she ever afterwards referred to him as "that horrid man". He also admitted he was not on good terms with Mr Thomas and claimed Mr and Mrs Thomas had not got on well together in their twenty year marriage, an admission pertinent to the rumour that Mrs Hearn had murdered Mrs Thomas so that she could marry Mr Thomas.

The chemist of the producers of the brand of tinned salmon from which the sandwiches were made gave evidence for the prosecution but Mr Birkett elicited from him testimony that while sterilisation of food by heat might kill the bacteria, food poisoning by toxins might still occur. The chemist also agreed that eating food in which there were toxins of a group commonly associated with tinned food, would manifest itself from two to four hours later. He agreed that cases of food poisoning could occur in which one person is affected but not others, even though they had all eaten the same food. One form of food poisoning, botulism, could produce peripheral neuritis.

Mr Birkett skilfully questioned the other experts brought by the prosecution to satisfy the jury that Mrs Thomas suffered initially from food poisoning and only later from arsenical poisoning for which others could have been responsible.

The Senior Home Office Analyst, Dr Roche Lynch, gave evidence for a whole day. Mr du Parcq questioned him on his expert knowledge of the effect of arsenic on human organs. Dr Lynch was of the opinion that Mrs Thomas had ingested two doses of arsenic; one in the sandwiches, a large dose of 14.3 grains; and another dose a day or so before her death. He said Mrs Thomas's liver would not have contained arsenic if it had been given more than a day or so before her death as the liver would have cleared it. He said white arsenic is tasteless and would not have been detected in the sandwiches. He had himself made a sandwich to test the point. Referring to the weedkiller that

Mrs Hearn had bought, Mr Birkett pointed out that it was blue and asked Dr Lynch if that weedkiller would have stained the sandwiches blue. Dr Lynch confirmed that if that weedkiller was put in a sandwich it would stain the bread and all the sandwiches would have been stained blue equally or at least have had blue spots. He agreed that the tablets at the farm used for worming animals could be taken in mistake for Genasprin.

Under Mr Birkett's questioning Dr Lynch had to admit that he had never seen a living patient suffering from arsenical poisoning. His knowledge was confined to organs removed after death had taken place. Dealing with the evidence Dr Lynch had given of his findings of arsenic in the body of Lydia Everard (Minnie), Mr Birkett was able to establish that the earth in Lewannick churchyard yielded, on analysis, a high proportion of arsenic but apparently no higher than might be expected in an area where there were tin mines. Some of the arsenic might have seeped into the coffin and impregnated the bodies after burial. Mr Birkett asked whether the water supply at Trenhorne Farm contained traces of arsenic but no tests had been conducted.

Police Superintendent Pill gave evidence of Mrs Hearn's arrest and the statement she made to him. In answer to Mr Birkett, Superintendent Pill said that the only arsenic police enquiries had been able to discover was the weedkiller Mrs Hearn had bought in 1926. When he had questioned Mrs Hearn he had found her to be cool and ready to answer. He said she appeared genuinely anxious to assist them.

Police Sergeant Trebilcock, who knew Mrs Hearn in Lewannick, gave evidence that when Superintendent Pill was writing down her statement, she turned to him (Trebilcock) and said in a low voice, "Mr Thomas used to come to the house every day with a paper. Of course, it was only a blind". Police Superintendent Pill had given evidence that he had not heard the alleged remark. Mr Birkett put it to Police

Sergeant Trebilcock that what Mrs Hearn had actually said was, "Mr Thomas used to come to the house every day with a paper. Of course, he was very kind" but the sergeant refused to admit that he could have misheard a remark made in such a low voice that the Superintendent did not hear it nor did another officer present with them.

Mrs Hearn was the only witness called by Mr Birkett. In spite of her mousey appearance and glasses, the 46 year old proved to be an impressive witness. She spoke in a straightforward manner about her early life, marriage, and sister's illness. She denied giving poison to Mrs Thomas or to her sister. She said she had given the leftover sandwiches to her dog which was not ill afterwards. Explaining her "flight" to Torquay, she said she had intended to throw herself off the cliff at Looe but found she could not bring herself to do so. Her testimony was unshaken when she was cross-questioned by Mr du Parcq.

On re-examination by Mr Birkett she said no-one had ever suggested until this time that she might marry Mr Thomas. Asked outright if she had killed Mrs Thomas in order to do just that, she replied to Mr Birkett that there was not an atom of truth in it. She had never conceived a passion, guilty or otherwise, for Mr Thomas. In order to be the last one to make a speech to the jury, except for the judge's summing up, Mr Birkett decided to call no further witnesses for the defence.

On the seventh day of the trial Mr du Parcq had started his closing speech for the prosecution when he suddenly collapsed. He was helped out of court by Mr Birkett to an ante-room where he fainted. The trial had to be adjourned but two hours later Mr du Parcq was able to return to the courtroom and continue his speech.

When Mr Birkett stood to begin his closing speech he started by paying tribute to the prosecutor saying, "The case here for the Crown has been presented by him with conspicuous fairness". In his biography of Norman Birkett, Montgomery Hyde writes that before coming into the court Mr Birkett had given some thought to his closing argument.

At first he thought of building it around a quotation from the 14th chapter of St John but he decided to discard this when he heard that the jury on the previous Sunday when given the choice of attending divine service or going for a motor drive had unanimously plumped for the drive. Eventually he took his cue from a shaft of sunlight which penetrated the windows of the court room. "For over five months, Mrs Hearn has lain in Exeter Gaol", he said, "When the darkness of winter has now come to this lovely light of this June day, for her upon trial for her life it may be said with truth she has been walking in the valley of great shadows. It is your hand and your hand alone which can lead her forth into the light."

For almost four hours Mr Birkett analysed the prosecution case and said it was fantastical to suggest Mrs Hearn had murdered Mrs Thomas in order to marry Mr Thomas. He said the Crown's case rested on the sandwiches being poisoned but there was no evidence for this; and that if they had been poisoned, the bread would have turned blue. He said Dr Roche Lynch, the Home Office Analyst, had never attended one living patient suffering from arsenical poisoning but he spoke of the symptoms with the same confidence he spoke of other matters. There was no evidence that weedkiller had ever been taken to Trenhorne Farm, the Thomas' home, but there were Cooper's worm tablets in the house which could be mistaken for Genaspirin. The worm tablets contained not only arsenic but also copper which the weedkiller did not contain. "And in the organs of Mrs Thomas there was found copper", Mr Birkett said. "Your verdict ought to be and should be that she is not guilty. For that verdict I appeal."

Mr Justice Roche summed up for the jury, telling them they were not trying Mrs Hearn for the murder of her sister. The prosecution had been allowed to try to show Miss Everard had died because poison was administered to her, they say by Mrs Hearn, in order to show that there was no accident or suicide in the case of Mrs Thomas. The judge told the jury to ask themselves two questions: was Mrs Thomas's death caused by arsenical poisoning? If they thought it was, then the second question was: was it the act of the accused person?

In reviewing the evidence, the judge said Mrs Hearn was an excellent nurse and had been a devoted sister. Minnie was delicate and ailing. He dismissed the idea that Mrs Hearn's motive could have been that she was tired of nursing Minnie who was another mouth to feed and an impediment to Mrs Hearn taking in lodgers to improve her finances. The judge said that if they were not satisfied arsenic was in the sandwiches they were to acquit. He examined the possibility that Mrs Hearn and Mr Thomas might both be guilty but pointed out that both had been investigated by others long before the jury and their silence on the question ought to make the jury hesitate long before they accepted such a suspicion or theory. Mrs Hearn's note left the balance of her money to Mr Thomas and not to her sister, Mrs Poskett, who had been helping Mrs Hearn financially. While it was usual to leave money to relatives it was not evidence of a guilty passion that Mrs Hearn paid Mr Thomas first. If they thought Mr Thomas guilty, what motive was there? There was no evidence of another woman and no money was involved as Mrs Thomas left only £100.

The jury retired for 54 minutes before bringing in a verdict of "Not Guilty" on the charge of murdering Mrs Thomas. The judge ordered that the case of Minnie Everard, with whose murder Mrs Hearn was also charged, would not proceed. Mr du Parcq offered no evidence for the Crown and the judge directed the jury to return a verdict of "Not Guilty".

The judge said to Mrs Hearn, "Sarah Ann Hearn you are discharged". Supported on one side by a nurse and on the other side by a wardress, Mrs Hearn walked out of the court and was never seen again.

It is believed she changed her name and returned to the North of England. She never returned to Trenhorne House. The contents, including a piano and a violin, were auctioned off to a crowd who packed every room for the viewing.

As there was insufficient evidence to charge William Thomas with the murder of his wife the case remains unsolved. After the verdict Mr Thomas left Trenhorne Farm and took another farm in a remote location where he lived as a recluse until 1949.

By the mid 1990s the half of Trenhorne House in which Mrs Hearn had lived had become badly run down. New owners bought it and restored it.

CHAPTER 5

Mylor: A Heart of Stone

O n 17 June 2004 a white dinghy, *Izz Wizz*, was found floating in Mylor harbour with the key in the ignition and no sign of the owner, Peter Solheim, a 56 year old Budock parish councillor who lived at Carnkie. Peter Solheim was last seen getting into his boat in Mylor harbour on the previous day, accompanied by another man who has never been found or identified. He had talked about travelling abroad with a friend, Charlie, who owned a bigger boat. The next day fishermen trawling off Black Head on the Lizard peninsula netted a body which proved to be that of Peter Solheim. At first it was thought that he must have fallen overboard from *Izz Wizz* but a post-mortem examination found that although he had died of drowning only a few hours before he was found, he had injuries which could not have been sustained in a drowning accident. Coastguards pointed out that it was impossible that he could have fallen from his boat in Mylor harbour and drifted to Black Head on the natural tides, drifts and currents. The police launched a murder enquiry and uncovered a web of sex, witchcraft, greed and jealousy.

As the police established Peter Solheim's mode of life they learned that he was a divorced man with a great interest in paganism and black magic. He dealt in pirated hardcore pornographic DVDs and antique firearms. His own collection of firearms was worth £30,000. He had been a Druid but gave it up to become a Wiccan.

A new bridge over the river Budock was built to replace an old clapper bridge. When his mother's house, next to the clapper bridge, was flooded on two occasions Peter Solheim was convinced that the flooding was brought about by the spirits of the river as a punishment for him. He wanted the old bridge used instead of the new one and he joined the parish council to try and bring this about.

Peter Solheim had been born and brought up in Budock Water by his mother while his father was away at sea. He was the only child of a Norwegian Chief Engineer on a whaling ship, which led in later life to his having a deep interest in Viking gods and his insistence on wearing a horned helmet, metal breastplate and double-edged four foot long sword over the plain white robe that was the dress the Wiccans wore. He told the local group of Wiccans that he wanted to be known as Thor's Hammer. One pagan priestess said Peter Solheim thought himself irresistible to women.

He took early retirement from his job with a printing company in the mid-nineties. He had two children from his marriage but after the divorce they chose not to have contact with him. His daughter said he had a fiery temper. Others said he was difficult and unpopular.

In 1995 Peter inserted an advertisement in the lonely hearts column of a local newspaper. Among the replies he received was one from a 47 year old widow living not far away. Margaret James was petite, 5'3" tall, and shared his passion for paganism. She told the police that in the early days of her relationship with Peter Solheim they ended up going to bed and "to coin a phrase, we were at it like rabbits". Her husband had died in a fire at a gravel pit and with the compensation she bought a former coastguard cottage on the cliff above the hamlet of Porthoustock. She supported herself on a widow's pension sup-plemented by selling mobile phones and SIM cards through free advertisements in the local paper. Margaret James was said to be greedy for money and for sex. A bicycle-riding vegan who enjoyed swimming naked in the sea, she had a son and a daughter from her marriage and two grandchildren. Both her children had been in trouble with the law and the son was in Dartmoor Prison at the time of Peter Solheim's murder.

The inquest revealed that Peter Solheim had been tortured for two days before being thrown into the sea. The cause of his death was drowning but his body had twenty injuries inflicted before death. He had been drugged with Lorazepam, a strong sedative, and mutilated with an axe or a machete. His kneecap was shattered, there were cuts to his elbow, and his big toe was almost severed.

Margaret James and Peter Solheim were lovers for nine years but she did not trust the openly flirtatious man. She knew he had had a twenty year on-off relationship with thrice-divorced Jean Knowles of Par, near St Austell. Mrs Knowles accepted that Peter Solheim had other women. It did not bother her. "We each did what we wanted to do", she said. Margaret James was jealous of Mrs Knowles and once telephoned the older woman to tell her to leave Peter Solheim alone. In spite of this Jean Knowles and Peter Solheim kept in touch by telephone. They started seeing one another again in 2001 and having sex three or four times a month. Sometimes he spent the night with her. By 2003 he had decided to marry her and bought an engagement ring which he asked her not to wear "until the time is right". He told Jean Knowles, "the muck will hit the fan" when Margaret James found out. On 15 June Peter Solheim made his last entry on his calendar, "Secret's found out", which the police took to mean he had either admitted his plans to Margaret James or she had found out.

From 17 June onwards Jean Knowles received text messages from Peter Solheim's phone saying he had met a friend named Charlie, they were going fishing and could be heading for France or Spain. She was suspicious because the text messages mentioned "Margaret" whereas normally Peter Solheim only referred to Margaret James as "M". Margaret James had also received text messages from Peter Solheim's phone. It appears she sent the texts to establish that Peter Solheim was alive and to lay a false trail. Unfortunately for her, the police were able to prove that the texts that had been sent from Peter Solheim's phone had been routed through the St Keverne mast near Mrs James' home and were sent thirty-six hours after his body had been recovered from the sea off The Lizard. But for the chance finding of the body by the fishermen so soon after it had entered the sea, it could well have disappeared and never been found. Certainly that appears to have been Margaret James' plan.

When the police searched Peter Solheim's home they found that a safe was missing and that there was just £20 in cash in the house. During a search of Margaret James' house £900 was found hidden under a mattress with a note saying, "what goes around comes around". A note in Margaret James' handwriting was found listing lethal poisons and putting against each the amount needed for a dose to prove fatal. Later £24,000 was found in her mother's house. The police noticed how vague and unemotional Margaret James was during questioning. They arrested her but she was not charged until February 2005. The police were convinced it would not have been possible for the tiny woman to have manhandled the body of 5'8", eleven stone, Peter Solheim by herself but they searched for accomplices without success. Nor could they discover where he had been held and tortured.

Mrs James appeared at Truro Crown Court before Judge Graham Cottle on two charges; one of murder and the other of conspiracy to murder, in April 2006. During the trial Mrs James gave evidence intended to damage Peter Solheim's reputation. She claimed he was obsessed by black magic and pornography, and had, she said, forced himself on her a couple of dozen times.

The prosecutor, Sarah Munro, QC, told the jury, "the injuries were caused by blunt and sharp weapons likely to be an axe or a machete. The injuries had been deliberately targeted. You will have to consider whether this was done to make his suffering more severe or to ensure his movement was severely restricted." She went on to say, "Don't be fooled by this diminutive woman. In truth, she has a heart of stone".

Ronald Hutton, professor of history at the University of Bristol and an author of books on paganism and witchcraft, told the court of the extraordinarily large and impressive store of ingredients used to make spells and potions that was found in Peter Solheim's attic, together with more than forty books on different aspects of magic and witch-craft. He later told BBC News that it was a vast assemblage for casting spells, with almost no relevance to religion at all. It was all about power, about his ability to exert his will over others and over other things. Some of the spells he was attempting to cast involved trying to seduce women and trying to harm his enemies. Professor Hutton said it was very, very, unusual to find someone interested in witch-craft purely as a means of personal gain and for selfish reasons. He said he had met literally thousands of modern pagan witches and the deceased man was the first he had ever encountered who practised bad magic or in old-fashioned terms, black magic.

Halfway through the trial Judge Cottle ruled there was insufficient evidence to support a charge of murder and the trial proceeded with the charge of conspiracy to murder.

Mr Paul Dunkels, QC, defending Mrs James, tried to show she was not the only person with a motive to want Peter Solheim dead. He claimed Peter Solheim had received hate mail calling him a sex offender and said that there was evidence he had committed serious sexual offences in the past. He dealt in antique firearms, had an interest in illegal weapons, and kept a "realistic" air pistol in his Citroen car.

The prosecution told the court Margaret James and her accomplices were motivated by "hatred, revenge and a desire to get their hands on his money".

After deliberating for nine hours the jury of three men and nine women returned a unanimous verdict of "Guilty" to the conspiracy charge. Told by Judge Cottle that she had shown no remorse for her crime, Margaret James interrupted him by shouting, "I can't feel remorse for something I haven't done. None of this has anything to do with me. It's a gross miscarriage of justice". Judge Cottle told her that what she had orchestrated was a horrific slow death. Sentenced to twenty years' imprisonment, Mrs James was also ordered to pay £120,000 towards the cost of the prosecution. She was refused leave to appeal.

The police search for her accomplices continues. Detective Inspector Stuart Ellis said, in February 2009, "It has always been our case that there were other people involved in the murder of Peter Solheim and they have not yet been brought to justice. We still need to know what happened to him during the time between when he was last seen and when he was found in the sea." Crimestoppers offered a reward of £10,000 for information leading to the arrest and conviction of the person or persons responsible for the murder.

Police returned to Porthoustock on 31 March 2009 and searched two homes. Scene of crime officers, wearing white suits, wrapped a 19 foot boat in black plastic and took it away for forensic examination.

Two men were arrested in May 2009 but later released without charge.

CHAPTER 6

Porkellis: A Promise

In January 1962 Miss Rene Hargreaves, a 54 year old herdsman, was living in a remote cottage, Wheal Rock, in Porkellis, near Helston, with her friend, Miss Boston, and a lodger, Ernest Massey. Mr Massey was a 78 year old retired steelworker from Flixton, near Manchester. Miss Hargreaves had nursed Mr Massey's wife and before she died, Mrs Massey extracted a promise from Miss Hargreaves that she would take care of her husband for the rest of his days. In 1960, after Mrs Massey's death, Ernest Massey made a Will, written out by Miss Hargreaves, leaving all he possessed to her. If she predeceased him, the money was to go to Miss Boston. Neither lady had any idea how much – or as it turned out, how little – Mr Massey had to bequeath.

Mr Massey suffered from arthritis, insomnia and, with age, came to be a dirty old man in his person and in his habits. He was senile, difficult, unwashed, nosey and greedy for sweet things. If he found something sweet he would stick his fingers in, lick them and continue until he was stopped.

Mr Massey, called "Uncle" by Miss Hargreaves, received regular visits from his doctor. Miss Hargreaves wanted Mr Massey to go into a Home but he refused his consent. She wanted the doctor to get him admitted to the Geriatric Hospital at Barncoose, Redruth, but no beds were available. During one of the doctor's visits Miss Hargreaves enquired of him if there would have to be an inquest on

Mr Massey if he were to die suddenly. The doctor assured her it was unlikely.

On 19 January Mr Massey messed his bed. Miss Hargreaves changed the bedding and sent for the doctor who did not arrive that morning. Mr Massey had a bowl of soup and a bottle of beer for lunch and was then left alone for some time. At 3pm Mr Massey collapsed. The call for the doctor was repeated and urgency stressed. When the doctor arrived he found Mr Massey dead. The doctor estimated that death had occurred about two hours earlier. There was no sign of violence and the death was not unexpected. Miss Hargreaves told the doctor that the previous evening she had found Mr Massey sitting on the stone floor of the kitchen having fallen while searching for beer. Mr Massey appeared unharmed and had got up and put himself to bed. He had often fallen without hurting himself while searching for beer and sweet things. The doctor had not seen Mr Massey for two weeks and when he heard about the fall he was unwilling to sign a death certificate and reported the death to the Coroner.

During his post-mortem examination Dr F D M Hocking, the Cornwall County Pathologist, found there were no visible injuries internally or externally. There were no bruises. What stood out for the pathologist was the fact that everything internal was a dusky-brown colour; a recognised result of poison by a group of drugs that change normal blood pigment (haemoglobin) into a brown variety (methaemoglobin).

A search of Wheal Rock cottage uncovered no drugs or photographic chemicals such as would cause the effects found. A tin of sodium chlorate was found in an outhouse with some of the contents missing. The marks on the tin lid indicated it had been opened several times. Tests on Ernest Massey's internal organs showed they contained sodium chlorate, which Dr Hocking estimated had been ingested within twenty-four hours of death. He also concluded that a number of small doses had been given to Mr Massey. A large dose would have been detected by the salty, unpleasant taste. Mr Massey had no history of gastro-intestinal illnesses, again suggesting very small doses which would be undetectable in beer or soup.

Miss Hargreaves told the police she had bought the sodium chlorate three weeks earlier to treat an overgrown garden path. She told Detective Superintendent Roberts that Mr Massey had become an increasing nuisance because of his senility and filthy habits. She had made repeated attempts to get him moved to a geriatric hospital without success. The situation had become increasingly desperate and she had put a little weed-killer in his tea with the intention of making him ill so that the hospital would have to take and keep him for the rest of his life. She gave him small doses with the intention of making him ill, not to kill him.

Miss Hargreaves did not realise that sodium chlorate is a slow-acting poison which does not show its effects for several days. Seeing no immediate result from the dose she had given him she continued to give him small amounts until his final collapse.

Miss Hargreaves was charged with murder. At Helston Magistrates' Court, on 27 January, Miss Hargreaves withdrew her confession and pleaded "Not Guilty". She was committed in custody for trial at Winchester Assizes where she appeared in April 1962.

Detective Superintendent Roberts, Head of Cornwall CID, told the court that a mug was found containing sodium chlorate in beer dregs. Miss Hargreaves at first claimed she "did not see how it could have got in the mug. He was a confounded old nuisance but if I wanted to get rid of him I would not have done it that way". Later Miss Hargreaves told the Detective Superintendent, "On the Wednesday before he died he really played me up. He let the fire go out three times that day. I lost my temper with him. I did it. I gave it to him about 9 o'clock in a cup of tea. I thought it would make him ill not kill him".

Mr Massey was known to steal food. Sugar and sweet things had to be locked away from him. Mr Norman Skelhorn, QC, for the defence, suggested Mr Massey might have found the tin of sodium chlorate, opened it and thought it contained sugar, as sodium chlorate crystals look like granulated sugar. He suggested Mr Massey put the poison in his drink in mistake for sugar. Mr Skelhorn then called Mr John Charles Walker, the manager of a Helston chemist, to confirm that sodium chlorate was not treated as a poison. There was no warning on the label that it was dangerous to people or animals.

The jury found Rene Hargreaves guilty of manslaughter. When the verdict was announced she collapsed in the dock. Mr Justice Finnemore said to her, "The jury have taken the view that you did not intend to kill this man or do him any grave harm. But there is no doubt that you did intend to do him some harm". He sentenced her to eighteen months' imprisonment.

Mr Massey left life insurance policies in his Will, the fully paid-up value of which totalled just under £150.

CHAPTER 7

St Austell: Mad or Bad?

Miles Giffard appeared to have it all. Good-looking, charming, educated at Rugby and Blundell's schools, Cornwall County cricketer, and elder son of a prosperous solicitor and his socially accomplished wife. Charles and Elizabeth Giffard and their two sons lived in a fine house, Carrickowl, built on the cliff top at Porthpean, overlooking St Austell Bay. Behind these appearances lived a very unhappy young man. It was said that his formative years had been scarred by a sadistic nanny who beat him and locked him in a dark cupboard. The sadistic nanny was sacked. The new nanny found that Miles suffered from dreadful nightmares and continued to do so for the years she was with him. It is likely his father's very strong personality and certainty in his own rightness played a part in forming Miles' character. Charles Giffard was a hard, unsympathetic man, overbearing and brusque, and he was reputed not to suffer fools gladly. Miles was quite unable to live up to his father's expectations of him.

Charles Henry Giffard had served in the Royal Flying Corps during the First World War. On marriage he and his wife made their home in the St Austell area. He was the managing partner of a firm of St Austell solicitors and had been Clerk to the St Austell Magistrates for twenty-three years. He had been Superintendent of the Special Constabulary for the mid-Cornwall area during the Second World War. To his friends at the Golf Club or his local, the White Hart, St Austell, he was "Charlie". Elizabeth Giffard was Vice-Chairman of the St

Austell Conservative Association and President of the Conservative Women's Association. She played bridge two or three times a week with her friends and was well-liked by all who knew her.

Miles was born in 1927: his brother, Robin, three years later. Robin appears never to have caused his parents a moment's trouble. At the time of Miles' trial, Robin was in Kenya working with an uncle and was unable to return to England in time to support his brother.

When he was 13 years old Miles was sent to Rugby school. After four terms the Headmaster consulted with the parents about Miles' behaviour. The boy was much more than usually dirty and untidy. He screwed up his bed sheets with his hands and bit holes in the sheets an inch or two in diameter. The parents withdrew Miles from Rugby and sought the help of a psychiatrist, Dr Roy Nevil Craig. Dr Craig found that Miles suffered from paroxysms of fear for no apparent reason. He told lies more often than the truth, and such lies were purposeless. Dr Craig diagnosed Miles as suffering from a rare form of schizophrenia which attacked young people; it was a mental disease of the utmost gravity and from which no recovery was possible. Dr Craig said he had been doubtful, at first, about diagnosing schizophrenia because he knew of no constitutional link but the hereditary link was provided when Charles Giffard had a mental breakdown, which was partly due to working too hard. Miles' treatment was stopped after two years because Dr Craig found that deep down in the mind was a condition too grave to continue any longer; it was not safe to ease the underlying difficulties. Dr Craig testified at Miles' trial that he had warned Mr Giffard that Miles was deteriorating and something should be done.

Miles was sent to Blundell's school in Tiverton, Devon. Although said to be cheerful, he was also a boy quite unlike the others. On one occasion he stuck a knife in his leg in a rage and seemed surprised that it hurt and was bleeding. He was, however, very good at games, particularly cricket. He played for the School's First XI in his final term and wanted to be a professional cricketer but his father would not hear of it.

Miles did his National Service in the Royal Navy between 1943 and 1947, spending three happy years as an able seaman. He adapted well to the discipline and service life. His self-confidence grew. He was an excellent sailor, well-mannered and liked by all. He might have had a happy life had he stayed in the Royal Navy but when his National Service was completed he returned home. His father wanted him to become a solicitor but had to concede it was a hopeless ambition for Miles. Miles twice played cricket for the Cornwall County Cricket Club in the 1948 Minor Counties Championship. The only thing he was good at was sport and his father would not entertain the idea of Miles becoming a professional cricketer. So Miles did a number of low-paid jobs, none of which he kept long. He took to drinking more than was good for him and his father lost patience with him and told him to leave home. Miles left but returned when his parents were out to steal his mother's jewellery which he sold. Charles Giffard did not report the theft and Elizabeth persuaded him to give Miles one more chance. Miles agreed to try working in his father's office.

In 1951 he was left a legacy of £750 and left home, going to live in Bournemouth. The money did not last long and he had to take low-paid jobs to support himself. He returned home but two months later went to London and rented a furnished room in Walpole Street, Chelsea. Miles soon lived beyond the £15 a month his father allowed him and took to borrowing from friends and to bouncing cheques. He met a 19 year old girl, Gabriel Vallance, and her mother. They both took a liking to Miles and he was often invited to their home in Tite Street. In an effort to impress them, Miles spent money he did not have, taking them to restaurants and theatres. Gabriel wanted Miles to break with his family and find a job in London with which he could support himself. When Gabriel tried tactfully to get Miles to smarten up his untidy appearance, he realised that as he had no money to buy new clothes he would have to go home to get a fresh wardrobe. He left London at the end of October 1952, hitch-hiked to Cornwall and arrived home on Sunday, 2 November.

Twenty-six year old Miles telephoned Gabriel to tell her his father would not allow him to go back to London. He insisted it was time for Miles to settle down, live within his means, stay in Cornwall to work in the family's solicitors firm, and abandon all ideas of playing sport for a living. Miles was desperate. He was sure Gabriel was the love of his life and wanted to be near her to fend off his rivals. On 3 November he wrote to her:

> *I have had a terrible row with the old man made worse by the fact that as usual he is right. Anyway the upshot is that he has forbidden me to return to London, at any rate for the time being. He says he will cut me off without the proverbial penny, so there does not seem to be any alternative until I can get a job. I shall not be able to take you to Twickenham, who will? I am terribly fed up and miserable as I was especially looking forward to seeing you tomorrow, and now God and the old man (hereinafter called the OM) knows when I shall. Short of doing away with him, I see no future in the world at all. He has stopped my allowance, anyway, and is giving me a pint of beer and twenty cigarettes a day, and has said "No pubs". No doubt your mother would approve. Give her my love and tell her that when she sees me I shall be a reformed character (nominally anyway).*

The Giffards had two cars. His wife had a Standard 8 and Charles Giffard drove a Triumph with the registration number ERL 1. He had had the number plate some time and transferred it to each new car he bought. On Friday, 7 November, Mrs Giffard took her husband's car and drove to a local Conservative branch meeting held in Plymouth. Miles and his father used Mrs Giffard's car to travel to St Austell. They returned home for lunch, after which Mr Giffard returned to the office for the afternoon. Barbara Orchard, the 19 year old live-in housemaid at Carrickowl, left the house at about 2.15pm for her afternoon off, and Miles was left alone in the house. He spent the afternoon curled up reading a book but his mind must have been on his desperate need to see Gabriel. He drank half a bottle of whisky before telephoning her at 5.30pm and saying that he might be coming to London to see her, probably on Saturday morning, but he was not sure. He said he was going to borrow his father's car and would telephone her later.

Charles Giffard arrived home around 7.30pm and his wife a few minutes later. As his father was getting out of the car Miles hit him repeatedly with an iron pipe. The lining of the car door was torn by a blow that missed its target. Another blow caught Charles Giffard on the arm he had raised to protect his face. Blows to the right side of the head knocked him unconscious. Mrs Giffard had parked the Triumph and gone indoors. She could not have known what was going on in the garage beside the house or she would have tried to stop it. Miles followed her into the house and struck her from behind until she was unconscious. Miles rang Gabriel to say he would be coming to London. He returned to the garage and, finding his father alive, struck him several times with the iron pipe, causing Charles Giffard to die. When Miles returned to the kitchen he found his mother was recovering consciousness so he hit her again. He fetched the large, wide, metal garden wheelbarrow, put both bodies in and began pushing it through the garden towards the cliffs. The metal wheelbarrow was wide and could just take the two bodies but when Miles got to the garden gate the wheelbarrow had to be tipped sideways to allow it to pass through. In the process blood-stains were left on the ground. With Mrs Giffard's body on top, it was not easy to get at Mr

Giffard's pockets, so the bodies were tipped out and Mr Giffard's pockets rifled. Some small belongings were left on the ground including Charles Giffard's empty wallet.

Dr F D M Hocking, the Cornwall County Pathologist, later deduced that the rough track made the overloaded wheelbarrow so difficult to push that Miles put his mother back in the wheelbarrow, pushed it along a right-hand track off the path and threw her over the cliff. The wheelbarrow left only faint wheel-marks on the return journey. He then trundled the wheelbarrow along the path to the cliff edge and pushed his father and the wheelbarrow over the precipice. Miles returned to the kitchen to wash away the bloodstains before doing the same in the garage. At 10.15pm he drove the Triumph away from Carrickowl and on to London. En route he changed out of his bloodstained clothes and into clean clothes. He threw the two and a half foot long iron pipe, which weighed 3lb, into the river at Fenny Bridge together with some bloodstained clothing. Near Ilchester he picked up two hitch-hikers and took them to Chelsea. They noticed that he chain-smoked throughout the journey and seemed tense. They judged him to be "a very good sort of chap". Miles arrived at Tite Street at about 6am on Saturday and slept in the car for two hours before calling on Gabriel. He spent some time with her and her mother, before leaving, telling them he had a business appointment at 10am and would return for lunch. He went to Piccadilly Circus and sold his mother's jewellery for £50. This was the second time he had stolen and sold her jewellery. He phoned Gabriel to say he was unable to make it for lunch but would meet her at 2pm. They went to a public house in the West End. She noticed that he was very quiet. He asked her to marry him and she said she would if he got a proper job first. Later, after they had been drinking for a while, Miles asked her to come outside with him. He said he had done something terrible. "What, pinched your father's car?", Gabriel asked. He told her he had murdered his father and mother. Although he was very upset, she did not believe him. They went to The Prospect of Whitby public house in the East End for more drinks and were tipsy when he took her to her home in a taxi. Then he said, "I cannot see you any more". He gave her the number of his room at the Regent Palace Hotel, where he was staying under the name "Gregory", and asked her to ring him next morning.

When Barbara Orchard, the housemaid, returned to Carrickowl at about 10.15pm, after her Friday afternoon off, she heard a car being driven away and recognised the sound as the Triumph. She spent a few minutes saying "Good night" to her fiance before going into the house. The hall light was on and Mrs Giffard's shoes and handbag were in the hall. The coat Mrs Giffard had worn to Plymouth that morning was on a chair in the kitchen. Barbara Orchard saw that some coconut matting used to cover part of the kitchen floor had been moved, a rubber mat was damp and the floor looked as if it had been washed and left smeary. When she looked more closely she saw bloodstains on the floor and on the cooker. A scrubbing brush, usually left outside the kitchen door, was in the scullery sink. Finding no-one was at home, she rang two hospitals fearing one of the family had suffered an accident. She went to bed but did not sleep well. Very early the next morning, she went to her fiance's house and told him of her concerns about the Giffards. She had heard the Triumph driven away and felt sure Miles had taken it. Her fiance contacted the Giffards' gardener, Harry Launcelot Rowe, who got in touch with the police. Detective Superintendent Kenneth Julian was contacted at Bodmin and, on that Saturday morning, he and his Scene of Crime Officer, PC Max Mutton, drove to Carrickowl. The County Pathologist, Dr F D M Hocking was also called out and he joined the team of police at the house. The Triumph was missing but Mrs. Giffard's car was in the garage. Her car was covered in bloodstains inside and out. There was blood on the garage floor and a stain outside. They found a tuft of hair later identified as Mrs Giffard's.

The gardener noticed that the wheelbarrow was missing. The police found wheelbarrow tracks and a trail of blood which led out of the garden gate. They followed the trail along the public footpath to the cliff at Porthpean. Looking down to the beach 120 feet below, they saw the body of a man they were sure was Charles Giffard and nearby lay the wheelbarrow. They were not sure of Mrs Giffard's fate. They searched the clifftop and 200 feet away found more wheelbarrow tracks. At the edge of the very steep cliff they found bloodstains. On the beach they found Mrs Giffard's body jammed between rocks.

After the investigation of the crime scenes the bodies were taken for post-mortem examination. Dr Hocking found that Mr Giffard had died from at least five heavy blows to the head and was dead before he was thrown over the cliff. Dr Hocking found that Mrs Giffard had been unconscious but breathing when she was thrown over the cliff, and her death was caused when her head struck the rocks and her skull fractured. Mrs Giffard has suffered extensive abrasions over her body and limbs. Her wrists and an arm were broken which, in Dr Hocking's opinion, were caused when she fell face down in the kitchen.

The Metropolitan Police were contacted and asked to look out for the missing Triumph, ERL 1. It was found in Tite Street, Chelsea. When Gabriel and Miles returned to her home after their Saturday night out, she got out of the taxi and, as the taxi started to draw away, it was blocked by police cars. Miles was arrested by police officers and detained at Cannon Street police station on a charge of stealing his father's car.

The next morning, Sunday, Detective Superintendent Julian of Bodmin interviewed Miles. After cautioning him, he said that he was making enquiries into the death of Miles' father and mother at some time on 7 November. Miles interrupted him to say, "I know what you are referring to. Let us clear it up with as little trouble as possible. Will Gabriel be brought into this? I had a brainstorm". Miles was taken back to Cornwall and formally charged with the murders.

Miles appeared at St Austell Magistrates' Court on 10 November charged with the murder of his father, the man who had been Clerk to that court for so many years, and was remanded into custody. During his appearance Miles was given permission to apply for legal aid. In the event his uncle, General Sir George Giffard, offered to fund the defence. Mr W G Scown of St Austell, a solicitor who had known Miles for some years, agreed to act on his behalf.

On the afternoon of 10 November the Bodmin District Coroner, Mr E. W. Gill, opened the inquest into Mr and Mrs Giffard's deaths and adjourned it indefinitely after hearing identification of the bodies from another brother, Mr Campbell Walter Giffard, a London stockbroker.

Miles made a second appearance in St Austell Magistrates' Court on 19 November, charged with the murder of his mother. Detective Superintendent Julian told the court that on being told he was to be charged with the murder of his mother, Miles had said, "No".

Miles was brought before St Austell Magistrates Court on 12 December charged with the murders of his parents. After hearing evidence from witnesses, Miles was committed to stand trial at Bodmin Assizes. Mr Park, Miles' counsel, told the court that Miles would plead "Not Guilty" and that one of his defences would be that he was insane.

The trial opened before Mr Justice Oliver on 3 February 1953 with Mr J Scott Henderson, QC, for the prosecution and Mr John Maude, QC, for the defence. Charged with murdering Charles Henry Giffard, aged 53, Miles pleaded, "Not Guilty".

Mr Scott Henderson said the prosecution's case was that on 7 November Miles made up his mind to go to London to meet his girlfriend and, having no money or means of getting to London, he decided to kill his father in order to take his father's car and fulfil his wish to go to London. The prosecution acknowledged that Elizabeth Mary Giffard had also been murdered but explained that because the deaths were so closely linked, in considering whether the defendant killed his father a lot of facts would be heard concerning the death of his mother.

Mr John Maude opened the defence by saying that he would call no witnesses to contradict the prosecution charge of murder; everything in the deposition was accepted. The ultimate question would be, "Was Miles labouring under a defect of reason to such an extent that he did not know that what he was doing, killing his parents, was against the law?"

The test for insanity in British courts was "the McNaghten rules" which held it must be clearly proved that, at the time of committing the act, the party accused was labouring under such a defect of reason, from disease of the mind, as not to know the nature and quality of the act he was doing, or, if he did know it, that he did not know what he was doing what was wrong.

Gabriel Vallance was called as a prosecution witness. Mr Scott Henderson read out the letter from Miles and made much of the phrase "short of doing him in" to try and establish that the murder of his father was premeditated and not an impulsive act. Mr Maude asked Gabriel if Miles had seemed perfectly normal until he told her he had murdered his father and mother. She replied, "Yes, although he seemed very quiet". The judge intervened to ask if Miles had been quiet all day. "When I first saw him he was quiet," Gabriel said. The judge asked, "Does that mean unusually quiet for him?" The witness replied "Yes".

It was for the defence to establish the defendant's mental state at the time of the murder. Mr Maude called witnesses of Miles' time at Rugby and Blundell's schools; and then the psychiatrist, Dr Craig, who had treated him. Dr Craig told the Court of Miles being referred to him after he was sent home from Rugby and of his diagnosis of a rare form of schizophrenia. He testified that he had warned Mr Giffard two years previously that Miles was deteriorating. Dr Craig agreed with the prosecution that he had written to the Giffards' family doctor, Dr Hood, in 1941 saying, "The door which was closed is slowly opening toward the outside world. We have got to go on if we are to save him breaking down mentally in adolescence". Dr Craig did not agree with the prosecution's contention that Miles had recovered from the illness. He said it was the discipline and controlled way of life in the Royal Navy which enabled Miles to survive as long as he had. In Dr Craig's opinion, Miles was going through a schizophrenic episode when he killed his parents.

A Harley Street psychiatrist, Dr Arthur Picton Rossiter Lewis, who had examined Miles in prison on three occasions, was of the professional opinion that at the time of the murders, Miles was suffering from a defect of reason due to disease of the mind. He knew to some extent what he was doing but he did not know that what he was doing was wrong in either the moral sense or in the sense of it being against the law. The psychiatrist was sure there had been a schizophrenic episode.

The prosecutor asked if the psychiatrist was prepared to say, based on what he knew of the events of 7 November and what he had seen of the prisoner, that Miles was suffering from schizophrenia. Dr Lewis replied, "No, I should not be able to say that unless I had the earlier history". Dr Lewis said Miles suffered from a defect in his blood of the normal amount of sugar which would give rise to symptoms identical to schizophrenia.

Dr John Matheson, Principal Medical Officer at Brixton Prison, gave evidence that an encepholographic examination was carried out on Miles to determine whether or not the brain was functioning normally. The result did not indicate any gross abnormality. Miles had been deprived of food for 21 hours to see whether his blood sugar content would fall below the danger level. The judge asked, "What was the use of starving him? He was not starving on November 7, was he?" Dr Matheson replied, "No, but this is what the authorities lay down as being the way to make this test". It was Dr Matheson's opinion that Miles did not suffer from a mental disease. Cross-examined by Mr Maude, "Would you agree it looks irrational in this case for this man to murder his mother and father in order to see that girl?" Dr Matheson agreed, "You could take that view". Dr Matheson said Miles had spent his whole life hurting his parents very much indeed and it seemed to him the final act of violence was in keeping with the man's personality. He agreed that killing the parents to go and see a girl was an extraordinary thing to do.

The prosecution called Dr John Hamilton Hood of Truro, for twenty years the Giffards' family doctor, to rebut the psychiatric evidence. Dr Hood thought Miles to be "an idle, selfish little waster who cared for nothing but his dreams of being a professional cricketer".

After the defence and prosecution had made their closing statements to the jury, the judge summed up the case for them. He said, "The man who butchered that old man and old lady, if he is not protected by being insane in law, is a murderer. The defence is that, at the time these acts were performed by the man you are trying, he was, in the eyes of the law, insane. The defence did not pretend he did not do it. He himself had given a minute, meticulous and apparently accurate account of what had happened. The second question is whether, at the time he did these acts, he knew he was breaking the law. In that matter the burden lies not on the prosecution. It is on the defence to make it at least more likely than not that at the time he did the act, the accused was suffering from some defect of reasoning, due to some disease of the mind, that made it impossible for him to know that what he did was unlawful." The judge said half a bottle of whisky drunk on a Friday afternoon might drive a man to do things he would not otherwise dream of doing. He asked why a man who did not know what he was doing was wrong, would want to wash up and get rid of evidence. "If he sent the bodies over the cliff and hoped the sea would wash them away, or if he sent them over expecting the injuries they had suffered would be completely submerged in the wreck that would take place to bodies falling 120 feet onto rocks, in your view does that indicate he knew he had done wrong when he did that? It took Giffard a great deal of time and effort to dispose of his parents' bodies and wash out the kitchen and garage; and if he did not make a particularly good job of it, was it to be said that he was mad for trying? What motive could he have except to conceal what he had done? What motive was there for taking clean clothes except to conceal what he had done?" The judge directed the jury that they had to find only whether Giffard was guilty, or whether he was guilty but insane.

Thirty minutes later the jury brought in a verdict of "Guilty". Mr Justice Oliver pronounced the sentence of death. Miles was taken to Horfield Prison, Bristol, pending an appeal.

On 23 February 1953 *The Times* newspaper reported that the previous day Messrs Stephens and Scown, the St Austell solicitors who acted for Miles, stated that a member of the jury had written to the Home Secretary saying that he was convinced Miles was insane when he killed his father and mother. The juror added that because of a mis-understanding, the judge had not been informed. Mr Scown stated that a letter was sent to the Home Secretary eleven days previously informing him of the information received. A reply was received from the Home Office stating that the juror in question had already written to the Home Secretary. A Home Office official said the Home Secretary had considered all aspects of the case in arriving at the decision not to grant a reprieve. Asked about the suggestion that the verdict of the jury was not unanimous, the spokesman replied, "That point goes to the secrecy of the jury room, and we cannot comment on it".

Despite appeals made to the Home Secretary by members of the public, the Headmaster of Blundell's, and others testifying to the disturbed state of Miles' mind, the appeal was dismissed.

Miles Giffard was hanged at Horfield Prison on 24 February 1953.

General Sir George Giffard, Miles' uncle who had paid for the defence and appeal for his nephew, wrote a letter to *The Times* newspaper, which published it on 7 March, drawing attention to Miles' long history of abnormality and mental illness from the age of four; the fact that a specialist examined him when he was fifteen; and that his parents were warned of the possibility of a breakdown in the future. After he left the Royal Navy he began once again to show symptoms of mental illness, but his father was ill at the time and no treatment was administered, and it culminated in the grim events of November 1952. "It is impossible for any ordinary human being to know how the mind of another is working", he concluded, "and for a jury to be expected to decide on 6 February, how the mind of a man suffering from mental illness was working on the night of 7 November, seems to the ordinary layman absurd. To decide such a case by rules which in the light of present-day knowledge are admitted to be in need of revision, seems to me to be manifestly unjust".

CHAPTER 8

Seaton: Frenzy

In the middle of the morning of 9 October 1942 residents of Seaton, near Downderry, saw a young girl walking over the bridge across the stream carrying a child in her arms while another child with a bloodied head walked beside her. She was wearing a bathing wrap, her hands were bleeding and blood ran down her thighs and legs. The girl was recognised as Mrs Eva Sandeman's sixteen year old maidservant, Elsbeth Sheila Ferguson, and the boys as Mrs Sandeman's sons, Charles and his younger brother, James. The girl was taken to the nearby Pearce's shop where there was a member of staff qualified to give first-aid. The girl asked that someone go at once to "The Crag" to help Mrs Sandeman who was lying injured in the hall. She held out her cut and bleeding hands to Mrs Pearce and said, "Look, Margaret, what Mrs Sandeman has done to me". She told the people in the shop that Mrs Sandeman had tried to murder her and Charles as well. Mrs Sandeman had cut her hand and hit the boy. Charles asked her why she had hit his mummy. Elsbeth denied having done so. Later she told the bystanders that she had done so to protect the children. While the first aider attended to the girl's cuts and dressed the boy's head, a telephone call brought the police to the scene.

The villagers were very shocked. They had formed the highest opinion of 37 year old Eva Sandeman in the six months she had lived at "The Crag". She had moved from Scotland to be near her husband, Surgeon-Commander Charles Sandeman, who was stationed at HMS

Raleigh, the naval training base near Torpoint. Mrs Ferguson had
known Elsbeth since she was a child. Six months before the family
left Scotland Elsbeth was engaged as the family's maidservant and
moved to Cornwall with them.

Charles Sandeman was called to Pearce's shop that October morning
and, showing him her injured hands, Elsbeth said to him, "Look what
your wife has done". When he returned to naval duty Charles Sandeman took his two boys with him. After she had told the police how
Mrs Sandeman had attacked her at "The Crag", Elsbeth was taken to
Liskeard Cottage Hospital. The police went to the house and found
the body of Mrs Eva Sandeman lying in a pool of blood in the hall.
Against her right arm there was a billhook covered in blood and on
her left side a white-handled carving knife. A wooden handle which
belonged to the billhook was nearby her left arm as were a pair of
child's reins.

On 14 October Police Superintendent F Sloman went to Liskeard
Cottage Hospital and, in the presence of her father, took a statement
from Elsbeth. She said she was sweeping the stairs when Mrs Sandeman came in with the boys. James never liked being brought in at
that time and began to cry. His mother slapped him with her right
hand. Elsbeth claimed that as she picked James up, she thought Mrs
Sandeman was looking suspicious and saw she was holding the billhook behind her back. Elsbeth had noticed that the carving knife was
on the umbrella stand. As she picked up the little boy Mrs Sandeman
came towards her with the billhook in her right hand and struck the
girl. Elsbeth said she took the carving knife from the umbrella stand
and put it in the dining room drawer. The maid claimed her mistress
rushed at her and Charles came into the room screaming for his
mummy not to hurt Elsbeth. Mrs Sandeman then struck Charles on
the head. Elsbeth said, "Don't hit Charles" and Mrs Sandeman
screamed she was going to kill the children. The girl claimed she

caught the billhook with her hand. Mrs Sandeman took the billhook, the statement went on, and struck herself on the forehead above her nose, then again her left cheek. Her eyes went very white and she collapsed in the hall. Charles ran into the kitchen screaming and Elsbeth said she took him and James out on to the lawn in front of the house. Mrs Sandeman was lying on her back in the hall breathing heavily. Elsbeth claimed she could not understand why Mrs Sandeman attacked her as they had never had any argument.

The Cornwall County Pathologist, Dr F D M Hocking, had been called to the crime scene. In his biography, *Bodies and Crimes*, he describes what he saw. As well as the victim lying at the foot of the stairs in a pool of blood with the weapons nearby, he noticed blood-stained footprints leading from the hall to the kitchen and then to the dining room. Blood had dripped or spotted along the same route and into the open drawers in the kitchen and dining room. If Elsbeth Ferguson's story of self-defence was true, the drops of blood from the hall to the kitchen and dining room would be hers, blood group A. The drops of blood were type O, Mrs Sandeman's blood group, as were the drops found in the kitchen drawer and dining room drawer. Dr Hocking compared the pattern of the soles of the shoes the sixteen year old had been wearing with the bloody footprints in the hall, kitchen and dining room and found that they matched; the blood type was O, which proved that Mrs Sandeman was already gravely injured before the girl went to the kitchen, as he believed, to fetch the knife. He examined Elsbeth Ferguson's hands and found the cuts on them were not what would have resulted if she had been attacked with the blunt billhook but must have been caused by the blade of a knife being drawn across them when they were clenched.

Dr Hocking was of the opinion that the forensic evidence at the crime scene attested to a different story: that the girl, having collected the billhook from the cellar by the back door where it was kept, made a

frenzied attack on her mistress, slashing at her until the handle of the
billhook fell off. The evidence pointed to the heavily bloodstained
girl having run into the kitchen to fetch the carving knife and, finding
it was not in the kitchen drawer, going into the dining room, taking it
from a drawer there and returning to the hall to continue her attack on
Mrs Sandeman. The cuts on the girl's hands had not been made by the
billhook but were consistent with the girl having held the carving
knife in her hand as she stabbed her mistress. The woman's blood on
the handle loosened the girl's grip so that her hand slid down on to
the blade and was cut as she stabbed. Transferring the knife to her
other hand, she continued the assault.

Superintendent Sloman charged Elsbeth Ferguson with murdering
Mrs Sandeman and brought her before Liskeard Juvenile Court on 14
October 1942. Elsbeth's eyes were swollen with crying and she was
weeping as she appeared in Court. Her left hand was bandaged and
her right hand was in plaster. She was remanded until 5 November
and her father was granted legal aid.

At Liskeard Juvenile Court on 5 November she pleaded "Not Guilty"
to the charge that she had murdered her mistress by attacking her
with a billhook and a carving knife. Mr J F Claxton, prosecuting, told
the Court that Ferguson had returned to "The Crag" very late on
Thursday, 8 October, after she had been to a dance. The following day
she told a friend that there had been a row and she was leaving. In
fact she had been sacked and the prosecutor put forward the dismissal
as the motive for the murder.

Evidence was given of the girl telling those at Pearce's shop that her
mistress had gone mad, cut her, Elsbeth's, fingers and hit Charles. A
neighbour, Muriel Snell, told the Court that she had seen Mrs Sandeman on the morning of the 9th, walking along a path at the side of
"The Crag" to the back door. James was with her on reins and crying

as if he did not want to go in. Elsbeth's friend, Constance Beech, aged 14, gave evidence of being told that Mrs Sandeman had been waiting up in bed for Elsbeth when she got back from the dance. Elsbeth looked as though she had been crying when she related to her friend that she had had a row with Mrs Sandeman and was going home. Superintendent Sloman's evidence covered his investigation and the accused girl's statement.

Charles Stewart Sandeman said Elsbeth had been in their service for a year and there had been no trouble. The maid's relationship with her mistress was a normal one. The girl had never complained of anything his wife had done. The accused got on well with both children, although better with the younger one. Elsbeth was of a placid temperament and he had never seen her in a temper.

Dr W H Spoor of Saltash said he had treated the girl's injuries. The left hand was severely injured with cuts on every finger where they joined the hand. On the right hand were four parallel cuts on the index finger. The wounds must have been caused by a sharp knife.

Dr Hocking told the Court that Mrs Sandeman had received 126 wounds made by two different instruments. Some were made by a very sharp knife and had to have been inflicted after death because there were no bruises around them. The other wounds, which had bruises around them, had been made by stabbing actions with a much blunter weapon. The greater number of injuries had been inflicted before death. There were four serious injuries, any one of which might have been fatal. Injuries to Mrs Sandeman's back could have been caused by sweeping blows with the billhook while the deceased and the girl were face to face.

Dr Hocking said that when the accused's left hand was closed all the lower cuts on her hand were in a straight line. The cuts could not have been caused by the edge of the billhook but had been caused by the blade of a sharp knife being drawn through the hand.

Elsbeth Ferguson was sent for trial at Bodmin Assizes where she appeared on 4 February 1942 before Mr Justice Lawrence. The girl was ably defended by Mr C L Hauser, who put it to the jury that when she was attacked, Elsbeth wrenched the billhook from Mrs Sandeman and struck back. The fact that some of the wounds had been inflicted after death showed that the girl was in a frenzied state as a result of being attacked.

In his summing up for the jury, Mr Justice Lawrence reminded them that a girl of Miss Ferguson's age could not be sentenced to death.

Elsbeth Ferguson was acquitted of murdering Eva Sandeman but found "Guilty" of manslaughter. She was sentenced to five years' imprisonment and served her sentence. She is said to have died soon after her release.

The Lizard: The Spirit of Love

At about 5am on 16 October 1943 those on duty at the RAF Radar Plotting Station located in the Housel Bay Hotel on the Lizard Point in Cornwall, heard the sound of a shot, followed about one minute later by a second shot. The Station Commander, Flying Officer William Croft, was seen running from the summer-house in the garden and overheard telephoning the Duty Officer, allegedly telling him, "I have shot Joan".

Flying Officer Norman Page, the Duty Officer, and a sergeant ran to the summer-house, which stood on a cliff facing the sea, climbed through an open window and found the body of WAAF Corporal Joan Lewis, dressed in her uniform, lying on the floor in a pool of blood. It appeared she had fallen from a sofa. On a table near the body was a heavy Webley service revolver, number 132070.

The police were called to the Housel Bay Hotel, a luxury hotel which had been requisitioned for use by the RAF, and at 7am Superintendent Thomas Morcumb arrived with the Cornwall County Pathologist, Dr F D M Hocking. They examined the body and the summer-house. When evidence from the death scene had been collected, Joan Lewis's body was taken to the nearby RAF Predannack where Dr Hocking carried out a post-mortem.

The police learned that the 32 year old Station Commander, Flying Officer William Croft, had said that he and Joan had made a suicide pact because they felt they could not live without each other. Joan had shot herself twice but his nerve failed and he could not go through with it. Croft was a married man with a wife and two children living in Bath. He later told Superintendent Morcumb that after the first shot Joan Lewis told him to get help and he left the summerhouse for that purpose. As he went away from the summerhouse he heard the second shot.

Twenty-seven year old Corporal Joan Lewis, whose home was in Porthcawl, Wales, had been stationed at Housel Bay for some time before Croft arrived. They met at a beach party and were immediately attracted to one another. This blossomed into a passionate affair. Croft knew he should end it. Not only was he being unfaithful to his wife but he was breaking service rules which forbade fraternizing between officers and other ranks. When the officer in charge of the WAAFs at the Station tackled Croft about his affair, she told him it had to stop. It was intolerable for morale and discipline. She said one of them had to leave the Station. Croft put in for a transfer but his application was refused by higher authority. It was agreed Joan Lewis should be posted to another Station. She was allowed two days' leave before her transfer and spent them with Croft before returning to duty at Housel Bay on 14 October. She and Croft spent the evening in Helston and the night of the 15th together in the summer-house.

In conducting the post-mortem Dr Hocking found that when the first shot was fired the gun had been held five or six inches away from the tunic, not pressed against the chest as would be more likely in a suicide attempt. The distance of the gun from the body was indicated by the degree of burning of the material and the spread of unburned powder fanning out in a cone from the muzzle of the weapon. The bullet had not gone straight through the body in the firing line but struck the sixth rib which it had fractured. It deflected upwards, missing the heart, then went backwards, exiting at the side underneath the armpit. The explosion and subsequent bleeding severely damaged the muscle over the upper part of the chest that is used in raising the arm. This point became crucial when the defence tried to show that this was suicide not murder. The pathologist was sure that the shot to the head could not have been fired by the girl except in an unlikely and awkward way.

When Dr Hocking gave evidence at Croft's trial, Mr Edmunds, for the defence, put Dr Hocking through all manner of physical contortions to try and convince the jury that the girl could have fired the second shot. The second bullet had entered the skull from above and in front of the left ear, exiting level behind the right ear. The shot had been fired from the left. After she was shot in the chest she fell from the settee on to the floor and was lying or kneeling there when the second shot was fired through her head. Dr Hocking reported that normally the Webley revolver would have been used with 04.55inch diameter cartridges. On examination it was found to have been loaded with five cartridges of that size and one slightly smaller, 04.50, which were used with Smith & Wesson revolvers. Two 04.55 cartridges had been fired into Joan Lewis and the next was 04.50 which was in the firing position. The trigger had been pulled on it as was shown by an indentation on the cap and mark on the firing pin in this indentation. Because of its slightly smaller size, this cartridge had slipped slightly down its position in the cylinder, thus losing the impact of the striking pin and preventing the firing of the primer. Dr Hocking was of the opinion that this tended to confirm the suicide pact but did not alter the fact that Croft had shot the girl.

RAF Flying Officer William James Croft appeared at Helston Police Court on 16 November 1943 charged with the murder of Joan Norah Lewis. The prosecutor referred to letters between the lovers showing that Croft had been very jealous; very much in love with the girl and she with him. He was married and he regarded his marriage as an obstacle, which seemed to worry him very much. Both were dreading separation. When charged Croft said, "At this stage all I want to say is that I did not murder Joan Lewis. She shot herself twice. We had both agreed to commit suicide". Croft was sent for trial.

Flying Officer Croft appeared before Mr Justice Humphreys at Winchester Assizes on 4 December. Mr John Maude, KC, prosecuted and Mr Humfrey Edmunds, KC, defended Croft.

Flying Officer Norman John Page testified that when Croft spoke to him on the telephone and asked him to go to the summer-house, he asked if it was anything urgent and Croft replied, "I have killed Joan Lewis".

When Flying Officer Croft went into the witness box he told the jury that before joining the RAF he had been an administrator with the Post Office in Bristol, was married and had a wife and two sons living in Bath. He recounted his meeting with Joan Lewis and the passionate affair that followed. He said they had both been so unhappy at the thought of parting that they had discussed committing suicide by either jumping off the cliffs or by shooting. When he went to meet her in the summer-house on 15 October he took his service revolver from his quarters and put it in his coat pocket with the intention of it being used on himself, or her, or them. When they met, they smoked, talked and dozed. Joan Lewis woke at 2.30am and said they ought to return to the hotel. They did not want to do that and so they dozed again until 4.30am. Croft said he could not possibly explain his feelings at the time. Joan asked, "What about it?" "We were both very highly strung," he said. He got the revolver from his coat and put it on either his, or her, lap. "I think we were both scared of what was going to happen. We sat like that for some considerable time. I felt Joan's hand in mine and then the weight of the revolver was taken off my knee." The next thing he heard was a shot. The arrangement he had made with Joan was that "we should cross our hands and close our eyes and the first person who decided to do the shooting should take the revolver and do the shooting and the person who was left should do the same thing". When he heard the shot he jumped up quickly. Joan said, "Fetch some help quickly, it's hurting". He asked where it was and she said, "in my chest". He opened a window and got out of the summer-house. When he had gone a few yards he heard the second shot. "I took the pistol meaning to shoot myself but I could not do it." He explained that when he told Page he had killed Joan Lewis, he meant that he felt himself responsible for what had happened.

Letters that had passed between Croft and the girl were read to the jury to show the state of the couple's minds. The prosecution claimed it was his jealousy that was the motive for the murder.

In his final speech to the jury for the defence, Mr Edmunds told them that the crime of "jealousy" put forward by the prosecution did not exist. The proper word was "despair" at parting. As well as telling the jury of the suicide pact, the defence put forward the case that after Joan Lewis had fired the first shot to her chest, as she fell to the floor the revolver struck the ground and accidentally discharged the fatal shot.

In his summing up the judge explained to the jury how suicide was self-murder, and if the girl killed herself by shooting herself, she committed murder, and if the man was aiding and abetting her, he was as guilty of murder as if he had shot her himself.

After deliberating for twenty-five minutes, the jury convicted Croft of murder. Addressing Croft, the judge said, "The jury have convicted you on evidence which, in my opinion, leaves no room for doubt. My only duty is to pass on you the sentence which the law prescribes for the crime of which you have been found guilty". His Lordship then passed the sentence of death which Croft heard without any show of emotion.

His legal team appealed the conviction on several grounds; that the judge had misdirected the jury in not putting to them the possibility of an accident, and that the judge was wrong in his direction to the jury that the existence of a suicide pact meant that the survivor could properly be convicted of murder because the authorities had shown that the survivor had to be present at the time. If the appellant's explanation of the tragedy was the true one, he had left the summer-house when the second shot was fired. The prosecution countered that there was no evidence that after the first shot Croft told Joan that it was his wish that she should not die and that he too should not die. He did not urge her to go on and did not even take the trouble to secure the revolver before he left the summer-house.

The judgement of the appeal was that there had been no misdirection of the jury. Croft had got out of a window leaving a loaded revolver in the possession of the woman. That conduct was not a counter-manding to end the suicide pact. Croft's conduct was consistent with his having aided, counselled, procured or abetted the deceased within the definition of the law. The appeal was therefore dismissed. Croft's sentence was, however, reduced from hanging to life imprisonment. He served only a few years before being released.

In his autobiography, *Bodies and Crimes*, the County Pathologist, Dr Hocking, tells how a friend of his, Commander T E Stanley, told him of a sequel to the murder.

Towards the end of January 1978, my wife and I visited Cornwall to negotiate for the purchase of the Housel Bay Hotel on the Lizard. This was to be our "retirement home" and ongoing hobby in our new roles as hoteliers. During the period of handing over and actually taking possession of the hotel on 20 April 1978, we were informed that not only were we acquiring the fixtures, fittings and other hotel impediments, but also the hotel's ghost.

We were informed that the ghost of a young woman in WAAF uniform had been seen walking in the hotel gardens on numerous occasions (always in the month of October), seen by several people, both young and old alike; the girl was alleged to have been murdered by her lover in 1943 whilst billeted at the hotel as a member of the WAAF Radar Plotting team operating a small station at Bass Point (since demolished, but traces of the mast's base mountings are still visible). On seeking confirmation of the so-called facts, the actual story, well-documented in press reports etc., came to light and will no doubt form a major part of the story. I do not wish to dwell on that particular part, but relate two other incidents which took place later.

On 4 October 1978 a Mrs W from Stockport in Lancashire telephoned to book a single room for herself and a small lap-dog for a four-day "break". On arrival she proved to be a mature lady of some sixty years or so, and of ample proportions! October 1978 was favoured with exceptionally fine weather and the good lady spent many hours in the hotel gardens with a book and her dog. On the second day of her visit (6 October), at approximately 3.30pm, she appeared at the hotel reception desk in a very distressed condition. She had been weeping, and her expensive mascara cosmetic had suffered in a most obvious way. However, having composed herself with the help of my wife and a few well-directed dabs with a hand towel, she quietly told us the following story, after first telling us that she was a Medium! She had apparently been sitting on the garden seat in the lower part of the garden when she heard a woman weeping. Realising that it was of a "spiritual" nature, she entered into conversation with the unseen spirit, which informed her of the facts of the murder and identified herself as the young WAAF concerned and went on to say she was waiting for her lover (also her murderer) to join her, as he had promised when they had made their suicide pact in 1943.

Mrs W who had, she alleged, never before visited Cornwall, was so intent on giving me the information which she thought would be news to me, she obviously did not at any time realise that the event she was describing was in actual fact well and truly documented! However, she was allowed to go on thinking we knew nothing, and informed us that she intended to revisit the same spot at 9pm the same night, as she had made an appointment to "meet the girl there". I was asked to escort her down to the garden seat, now in pitch darkness, by the light of a torch. My instructions were to return in 15 minutes' time to observe her without actually distracting her from her trancelike state, and if all appeared to be well, I was to return again after a similar period of time had elapsed and remove her, by force if necessary, back to the hotel.

As it happened no force was required and she returned, albeit in a distressed state, weeping etc., to the hotel where she wrote down details of her conversation with the "girl". I was most interested and intrigued to read within her "report" dates, times, names etc., which I knew to be correct from the well-documented story which appeared in the press reports of 1943, although I am certain that Mrs W still had no knowledge of the true facts of the case. She returned to Southport ?
a few days later without further enlightenment. At all times she wished to speak only to my wife and myself about her encounter with the girl, and was not in any way desirous of making financial gain from her experiences.

The second incident occurred in August 1979, when a Mr and Mrs B arrived from Sheffield for an eight day holiday. Mr B was an artist, and his bread-and-butter work was designing murals in mosaic tiles for ceilings and walls of houses and palaces of sheikhs in the Middle East, a full time job but not as creative or diverse as he would have wished, apparently. In order therefore to fulfil his creative desires, whilst on holiday he insisted on carrying around with him, at all times, an artists' pad in which he sketched almost everything within sight! On the third day of his holiday, at about 2.45pm, he came up from the lower garden saying he had seen a young lady sitting on the lower garden bench seat dressed in a RAF blue uniform, skirt and blouse, looking particularly dejected and with a "faraway" look in her eyes, who appeared to be waiting for someone to join her. He commented on the fact that he could never understand why some of today's young people insisted on wearing articles of clothing from World War II, and enquired if the young lady was staying in the Hotel. I replied in the negative and gave the incident little thought.

The following day Mr B came to me again from the lower garden, and made further reference to the young girl, who he alleged was again sitting on the same bench as on the previous day. He had almost decided to speak to her, but something made him change his mind at the last moment and he continued to walk back to the hotel where, of course, he spoke to me again. It was at this stage, I suddenly recalled the WAAF incident and decided to see the girl for myself, but, on reaching the bench seat, I found it empty and decided not to mention anything of what I suspected to Mr B, except to say I thought he was pulling my leg about a pretty girl who just did not exist, as I hadn't seen her on the bench seat or even depart from the garden. He insisted that she had been in the seat and he would look out for her around the hotel.

The very next day at about 3pm he came up from the lower garden, again saying that the same girl was on the bench seat. I immediately went to see for myself but there was no sign of the girl when I arrived a few minutes later. I told Mr B that I was convinced he was "pulling my leg", and that no such girl had been seen, to which he replied, "Oh! Yes there was, because this time I sketched her", and he produced the sketch of the girl, tore it from his artists' pad and presented it to me — and I still have it in my possession.

Dr Hocking went on to say that he had seen the sketch. He added that "after this lapse of time, my considered opinion is that this was a tragic suicide pact that went wrong".

Tregonissey: Poison

W hen the Inquest into the death of Mrs Annie Black of Tre-
gonissey opened in St Austell Coroner's Court on 11
November 1921, only one witness was called. Marion Ivy
Nicholls, Mrs Black's 17 year old daughter, told the Coroner that her
50 year old mother was the wife of Edward Ernest Black, an insurance
agent, and confirmed that he was her mother's first husband. The
Inquest was then adjourned to await the report from the Home Office
Analyst following his examination of Mrs Black's internal organs.

Edward Black was born in Burnley, Lancashire, and moved to St
Austell at the age of 21 to work in the china clay industry. He married
Annie Nicholls, an unmarried mother, of Duloe on 4 August 1914. She
was fifteen years older than him and there was lively interest in the
disparity in their ages. For some years Annie Black had been a school
teacher until she took over the village shop in Tregonissey. Edward
Black was active in the local community; he sang in St Austell Choir
and assisted with first aid at local football matches. When he left the
china clay industry he was employed as an insurance agent by the
Refuge Assurance Company until he was dismissed on 2 November
1921. Marion Nicholls was hoping to become a teacher like her
mother. Until the time of her mother's death she had believed herself
to have been adopted.

Mrs Black's funeral took place in the absence of her husband, who
had been missing for some days. On the same day, 15 November, St

Austell County Court heard two charges against Edward Black of obtaining money by false pretences. Miss Norah Smith of Carpilla, Foxhole, sued Black for delivery of an insurance policy on the life of John Rowse in the sum of £50 which she said he had sold to her. She had lent Mr Black £15 on security of the Refuge Assurance Company policy and later gave him another £15. She never received the policy which proved to be non-existent. The Refuge Assurance Company sent a letter to the Court confirming there was no policy. The Deputy Registrar gave judgement to Miss Smith.

In the second case, Charles Snowden Smith, a Foxhole cooper, brought an action against Mr Black for the dissolution of a partnership between himself and Mr Black in regard to Cunard shares. He told the Court that in April 1920 Mr Black told him and his mother that he, Black, held Cunard shares which were paying 22½% dividend. He offered to let Mr Smith buy some of his shares for £20. Mr Smith parted with the money and at Christmas received £4.10s. said to be interest on the shares. Mr Smith was offered and bought another £20 worth of Cunard shares from Mr Black in March 1921. The original certificate of partnership between Messrs Smith and Black was amended to show the increase in Mr Smith's holding from £20 to £40. On 1 November 1921 Mr Smith sent Mr Black a notice to dissolve the partnership. After the summons was issued, Mr Smith received a letter from the Cunard Company, which he produced to the Court, stating that Mr Black was not on the Register of holders of stocks and shares in that company. Deputy Judge Lush, who heard the case, gave judgement to Mr Smith for £40 with interest due at 22½%. A warrant was issued for Mr Black's arrest on a charge of obtaining money by false pretences.

There was much speculation about Black's whereabouts. Ships at sea were contacted and Black's description sent to them in case he had signed on as crew or, in the case of liners, was a passenger. His description was circulated throughout the country and the police put on alert. He was described as 5′ 7″ tall, clean shaven, with black hair and brown eyes. He had a heart tattooed on his left wrist.

Before the warrant for Mr Black's arrest was issued, and before Lancashire police were on the look-out for him, he returned to his home town of Burnley where his mother and brothers were living. Two days after arriving he left before the police in Burnley knew he was wanted.

A second warrant was issued on 18 November for Black's arrest on charges of obtaining from George Moss, a coal store manager, by false pretences, two sums of £15 and one of £20 for the purchase of insurance policies which did not exist.

Joseph Kelly, a butcher in Tregonissey, received a letter from Black thanking him and others for arranging his home affairs for him. He was most grateful for their intervention and wanted his letter to be shown to them so they would know how grateful he was. He said he had nothing to do with his wife's death and had made a great mistake in leaving St Austell under the circumstances but he was innocent and would not be brought back to St Austell alive. The letter was shown to a number of people who noticed that the address was written as "Burnley" and that it had been posted in Southport. The letter was given to the police who refused to reveal the contents.

At midnight on 21 November the Liverpool police found Black. Claiming to be a commercial traveller from Preston, Black registered at Cashin's Temperance Hotel under the name of Stevens. The owner of the hotel started talking to him and judged him to be very friendly and genial. After they had had a long and agreeable conversation, Black went out to get a drink and the hotel proprietor picked up the evening paper. She immediately saw the photograph of the "Wanted"

Edward Black but found it hard to believe that he and Mr Stevens were one and the same. In spite of Mr Stevens having blue eyes and not the brown eyes described in the paper, she felt sufficiently confident to go to the local police station and make a report. When two policemen knocked on his bedroom door Black said, "Right. Wait a minute". When the door remained shut the police broke it open and discovered Black sitting on the bed with his hand to his throat and blood streaming down. The police sprang at Black who responded by struggling violently. He was overcome, arrested and taken to Liverpool Northern Hospital where he was treated and kept in. He was removed from the hospital on Wednesday, 28 December and placed in custody at the police Bridewell to await an escort to Cornwall. When Black appeared at St Austell Magistrates' Court on charges of defrauding George Moss, he had a moustache and a black beard and walked with a limp. His throat appeared to have healed. Observers thought he looked frail and ill as the police helped him into Court. During the hearing he was overcome by faintness and had to be revived with a drink of water. He was committed to stand trial at Bodmin Assizes for fraud.

When the Inquest into the death of Annie Black resumed at the beginning of January 1922, the Senior Home Office Analyst, Mr James Webster, told the Coroner that he had found arsenic in Mrs Black's organs. Evidence was given by the Manager of Timothy White and Taylor, Chemists, in St Austell, that on 29 October Black had bought two ounces of arsenic, claiming he needed it to rid his house of rats. Black had signed the chemist's book recording purchases of poisons.

Mrs Black's daughter, Marion Nicholls, told the Court there were no rats in the house. She told the Coroner her mother, who had enjoyed fairly good health but had suffered from indigestion, had been taken ill on 21 October. The doctor was called and prescribed for her before the patient took to her bed. The medicine was kept downstairs and given by Black to his wife. Miss Nicholls said relations between the Blacks were fairly good except on one occasion when there was a difference about money matters. At the time of the marriage Mrs Black had had £125 which Black took, supposedly to buy gas shares. Miss Nicholls had found out there were no gas shares but she had no idea what had become of the money. There were three insurance policies on Mrs Black's life, one in favour of Miss Nicholls and two in favour of Black.

Replying to a question from the Deputy Chief Constable, Miss Nicholls revealed that she had been having sex with Black since she was 15. She claimed he forced himself on her and the relationship continued because she was afraid of him. Fear had prevented her telling her mother what was happening.

Several neighbours gave evidence of repeatedly visiting Mrs Black, sitting up at night with her, and hearing her complain about the taste of the medicine.

After the jury had retired, Black, who had been observed to be looking ill throughout the hearing, asked to make a statement. The jury was brought back and, in a very low voice, Black told them he had never purchased arsenic, never signed the Chemists' poison book, and that the signature in the book was a forgery. He claimed that on the day he was said to have bought arsenic in St Austell he had gone shopping there with Marion and spent the whole time with her. The following day his wife was feeling better and they went out together.

The Coroner's jury returned a verdict of "Wilful Murder" against Black and later he was brought before St Austell Magistrates on a Coroner's Warrant to be charged with murder and remanded.

On 20 January 1922 the Director of Public Prosecutions, Mr J Vivian

Thomas, presented to St Austell Magistrates' Court hearing the prosecution's case against Black. In his opening statement he spoke of Black's purchase of arsenic, his telling neighbours that the doctor had said his wife's heart valves were gone and she was unlikely to recover, all of which was untrue; his opportunities to administer arsenic; his wife's complaining about the taste of the medicine when he gave it to her but not when neighbours did, and his motive. Black had a friendship with another woman, was in financial difficulties, and desired to free himself from the woman who stood in his way.

Marion Nicholls was the first witness and told the Court about her sexual involvement with Black over the past two years. Shown a Red Cross book which had the corners of two pages which dealt with the stomach, arsenic and arsenical poisoning turned down, Miss Nicholls said she had frequently seen the book in her home.

A travelling pedlar named Tomkin gave evidence that he had often seen Black at night with a Mrs Olver, whose husband was abroad. He identified photographs found on Black as being of Mrs Olver.

Dr E G Andrew denied the medicine he had prescribed for Mrs Black contained any arsenic and denied telling Black his wife's heart valves were faulty and that she was unlikely to recover. He had found Mrs Black to be much relieved when her husband went missing; and she had said that she felt much more comfortable than before.

Black was committed for trial at Bodmin Assizes where he appeared before Mr Justice Rowlatt on 1 February 1922. Mr H Gregory, KC, appeared for the prosecution and Mr Llind Pratt for the defence.

The Senior Home Office Analyst gave evidence that there was about one-sixth of a grain of arsenic in Mrs Black's body. In the fluid of one of the bottles and jars the police had removed from the Blacks' house and he had examined, he found a trace of arsenic but it was too small to affect the human system. Cross-examined, Mr Webster told the defence that arsenic is quite quickly expelled from the body and after a short time, although it would remain in the hair and nails for a long time. Mrs Black had had a diseased kidney which had been unable to do its work of expelling the poison properly.

Sir William Willcox, Physician to St Mary's Hospital, said Mrs Black's symptoms were entirely consistent with arsenical poisoning. He was of the opinion considerable doses of arsenic were ingested on 31 October. It was possible poisonous drugs were given in the first days of illness. He agreed with the defence suggestion that the symptoms of arsenical poisoning and gastritis were identical.

On the last day of the trial, following a suggestion from the jury, the Home Office Analyst was asked by the Judge to make three cups of tea; one containing two grains of arsenic; one with one grain of arsenic in it; and one with none. Mr Webster undertook to obtain some arsenic and make the tea. There was no arsenic to be found in Bodmin and Mr Webster was asked to go to Wadebridge by motor car to try and buy some there.

The judge in his summing up said that the case was built on circum-stantial evidence. Usually in such cases the motive became evident but no motive had been shown in this case. There was no doubt that throughout his wife's illness Black had shown attention to her and never neglected her or been hostile towards her.

Just before the jury retired, the Senior Home Office Analyst returned from Wadebridge with arsenic and made the cups tea as requested. He handed them to the judge and jury. The jury retired and deliber-ated for forty minutes before returning a verdict of "Guilty".

According to a report in *The Times*, Black took the verdict calmly. When asked if he had anything to say as to why sentence should not be passed on him, he gave no indication of having heard the question. Mr Justice Rowlatt immediately put on the black cap and without pre-amble pronounced the sentence of death.

There had been great public interest in the trial and much competition for seats in the public area of the courtroom. A crowd estimated to be more than a thousand people waited outside the Court to see Black's departure for the railway station en route to Mutley Prison, Plymouth, before being taken to Exeter Prison.

The charges of fraud in connection with insurance policies were allowed to remain on the files of the Court.

Edward Black's appeal against conviction was heard at the Court of Criminal Appeal. Mr Pratt argued for Black that Mrs Black was ill on 27 October, two days before Black bought the arsenic. The judge, in directing the jury, had ignored the daughter's evidence that her mother had not been well for a week before she began complaining of stomach pains on 27 October. Mrs Black was taken violently ill on 31 October and continued to be ill until 6 November when there was a marked improvement.

Black ran away on 8 November because he was in deep financial difficulties and anticipated being charged with fraud. Mrs Black was again taken seriously ill on 10 November and died the next day. Miss Nicholls was always in the house, neighbours were in and out at all hours but Black was not there. Sir William Willcox had admitted that the symptoms of gastritis and arsenical poisoning were identical. The medical expert understood that the difficulty for the case was the length of time Mrs Black had lived, combined with the amount of arsenic involved. The amount of arsenic was too small to be weighed and had only been found through the Marsh Test which itself was not a trustworthy test. Medicine, ointment and toothpaste found in the house all contained tiny quantities of arsenic as impurities of the ingredients. Black had left Tregonissey before 9 November. Administration of arsenic, accidentally or deliberately, on 9 November would account for the symptoms on the following day and Mrs Black's death on the day after. The cause of death was an improperly functioning kidney.

The appeal also considered that, as the prosecution made no attempt to establish a motive for murder, the judge had been wrong to bring to the jury's attention the difference in age between the couple. As he did so, he ought to have balanced it by pointing out that Black could have got rid of his wife by divorcing her or leaving her without the need to murder her.

The Court of Criminal Appeal dismissed the appeal and Edward Black was hanged at Exeter Prison on 24 March 1922.

The publicity surrounding her mother's murder, the sexual abuse she had suffered from her stepfather, and her illegitimacy, may be the reasons why Marion Nicholls gave up her plan to be a teacher and took over the running of her mother's shop in the village, among understanding and supportive neighbours.

CHAPTER 10

Wadebridge: Guy Fawkes' Night

The shots attracted no attention because it was Guy Fawkes' Night when Graham and Carol Fisher were savagely murdered in their bungalow near Wadebridge. Graham, 60, and Carol, 53, owned and ran the Perch petrol station for 25 years. On 5 November 2003 they had closed the garage after the day's business and gone home to the bungalow behind the garage.

Just before 8am the next day a school bus driver, who parked his bus on the garage forecourt, arrived to collect the bus for the morning run. He noticed that Graham had not removed the traffic cones which blocked the entrance and exit to the garage as he usually did by that time of day. The driver collected the bus and took the children to school. He returned just before 9am to park his bus and noticed that a window in the bungalow had been smashed and the curtains were flapping in the breeze. He went to investigate and found Carol lying dead on the path by the garden gate.

When the police arrived they found Graham lying in the kitchen. He had been shot once in the chest, once in the back, and bludgeoned to death with a blunt object like a sledgehammer. The television was on in the living room, a coffee table was set ready for a meal, and the oven was on at 140° with a pie cooked to a blackened crisp inside.

Detective Superintendent Stuart Newberry, who had more than thirty years' service with Devon and Cornwall Police, was put in charge of the case. The police were able to reconstruct that Graham and Carol had just sat down to start their evening meal and watch television when a heavy flower planter came through the lounge window and landed on the settee. Another flower planter was thrown at a bedroom window which remained intact. The kitchen door was smashed open and the shocked couple were confronted by two men, at least one of whom was pointing a shotgun. Carol Fisher reached for the telephone but as she dialled 999 she was shot in the hand and mis-dialled so that the call did not get through. Blood spattered the tele-phone. She ran, trying to escape her attacker, as was evidenced by the trail of her blood which splattered the walls as she ran. She had reached the porch when she was shot again in the back. She staggered 60 feet down the garden path before she collapsed and was bludg-eoned to death.

The level of violence against the Fishers shocked the local community and the police. Detective Superintendent Newberry later described the scene confronting his officers as "almost beyond belief". The bru-tality used caused the police to wonder if there was a personal motive for the murders but no evidence was ever uncovered to suggest that the Fishers knew their killers. The police suspected robbery must have been the motive for the attack but they have never been able to establish what, if anything, was taken. The couple's safe was lying open but about £2,000 inside was untouched. What had been in the safe before it was opened is not known. Detective Superintendent Newberry was to say later that if robbery had been the motive it was "bungled" because things which should have been stolen were not. Those who knew him were sure Graham Fisher would not have handed over the money.

When the police entered the bungalow they found it so packed with furniture and belongings that they were unable to conduct a search for evidence. "The scene itself was very difficult", said Detective Superintendent Newberry. "There was a lot of stuff in the place and it looked as though the Fishers had never thrown anything out. They seemed to save everything. There were some rooms you couldn't actually get into because of the sheer bulk in the way." The police had the bungalow emptied. Everything was taken to an empty hangar at RAF St Mawgan, some distance away, where each item was carefully examined in the search for clues.

There were no CCTV cameras at the petrol station or the bungalow; no unidentified fingerprints were found in the bungalow; there were no witnesses; the spent shotgun cartridges had been picked up by the perpetrators; and no motive emerged. The case became so complex that Detective Superintendent Newberry had to postpone his retirement by twelve months.

The murder was featured on the BBC's *Crimewatch* programme and a £10,000 reward offered for information leading to the conviction of those responsible.

Six weeks after the murders at Perch Garage, another armed robbery took place at the Kingsley Service Station, Fraddon, Cornwall, when £70 and a few cigarettes were taken. Unnecessary violence was used in the crime and a masked man, armed with a shotgun, blasted a hole in the garage wall. A forensic link found there became the turning point in the Wadebridge case.

Robert Firkin, 32, and his brother Lee, 30, were not hitherto known to the Devon and Cornwall Police or to the Somerset and Avon Police. Originally from Dagenham, Essex, they moved to Exford Close in Weston-Super-Mare, Somerset, in 2003 when, in their words, they were driven out of London by gangland bosses. They were arrested in connection with the robbery at Fraddon and, at the end of December, named as suspects in the Wadebridge murders.

Police enquiries met with silence from associates, relatives and acquaintances of the Firkins. People refused to talk, either from fear or from loyalty to the brothers, and the police had to detain some before they were willing to cooperate. As the brothers were 6 feet 4 inches and 6 feet 2 inches tall, ruthless and extremely violent, the reluctance to talk was understandable.

The police made a breakthrough on 29 December 2003 when they recovered a package which had been buried in the beach at Sand Bay, Weston-super-Mare; it contained a sawn-off 12 bore double-barrelled shotgun and a sawn-off .410 shotgun which were linked to the Firkin brothers by DNA evidence and by fingerprints. Forensic tests on the shotguns and police enquiries into the brothers' movements took time but in May 2004 the police arrested the Firkins at the prison where they were already on remand. Lee Firkins explained that the weapons were acquired after 5 November to protect him and his family from threats made to them which had forced their move to Somerset.

Robert Firkins was a juvenile when first convicted in 1989 for criminal damage. He went on to earn a record for theft, burglary, drugs and criminal damage offences. When Lee Firkins was still a juvenile he was convicted of causing actual bodily harm. He also had convictions for possessing an offensive weapon and for drugs. In 1997, at Chelmsford Crown Court, he received a sentence of four years' imprisonment for wounding with intent.

Both brothers denied being involved in the Wadebridge crime. They admitted robbing the Taunton B&Q store on 18 December 2003 and stealing over £2,500 in cash and vouchers. £1,500 of this was dropped by the fleeing robbers and found outside the store. Lee Firkins admitted armed robbery, with accomplices, at the Jet petrol station in Fraddon, where he fired a double-barrelled shotgun at the wall. The brothers also admitted slashing a man's face with a knife before squirting ammonia in his eyes, tying him up, and dumping him in the Cornish countryside. Robert and Lee Firkins maintained they had not murdered the Fishers. They claimed they had made the 140 mile round trip to buy cannabis and had spent the evening at the Grenville Arms, St Austell, but the landlady denied they had been there. Through mobile phone records the police were able to prove that the brothers had been together at the relevant times on 5 November 2003 and in the area of the Perch Garage.

The murder of the Fishers featured on the BBC's *Crimewatch* programme and gave the police what was to prove to be the most controversial evidence against the brothers. A career criminal with a drug habit, who shared a cell with Robert Firkins, informed the police that Robert had bragged to him, "Watch *Crimewatch* and you will see my work". He claimed that while he was walking around the exercise yard at Exeter Prison smoking cannabis, Robert Firkins and a group of prisoners were there. He said Robert confessed to him that they had done the killings. The informer said he was told the Firkins picked the Perch Garage because " it was in the middle of nowhere and looked an easy job". He told the police Robert had said the brothers were parked in a lay-by smoking crack cocaine when they saw a guy coming out of the garage heading towards the house with a money bag in his hand. "He was an old gent and an easy target." The informer claimed Robert Firkins told him Mrs Fisher tried to run away but they caught up with her. Lee Firkins took off his balaclava and they smoked more crack cocaine while they decided what to do. They shot the couple again before running out of cartridges and "finished them off with a cosh". "We do not do things by half measures, we do a good job."

At a trial at Exeter Crown Court in November 2005 before Mr Justice Owen, the Firkins were charged with the robbery of the B&Q store, the Fraddon robbery and the attack on the St Dennis man. They pleaded

"Guilty" to those charges. In reply to the charge relating to the killing of the Fishers both brothers answered, "Not Guilty". The prosecution had to rely on evidence that the brothers were in the Wadebridge area at the crucial time, their ownership of the shotguns, the confession to the cellmate, the propensity for violence and the string of similar offences.

The informer repeated to the court the account of Robert Firkins' confession to him. He said Robert had told him that Lee was going to "take all the heat" and "take the rap". Cross-examined by Mr Mukul Chawla, QC, for the defence, the informer denied that he had made up the allegations because he wanted the £10,000 reward.

Stephanie Best, who was a witness in the case of the St Dennis man, told the Court that she was in the house when the brothers made their attack on Martin White and had heard one of the brothers, she was not sure which, mention Wadebridge.

The Home Office Pathologist, Dr Gyan Fernando, told the Court that Graham Fisher had been shot three times and his skull fractured into two pieces by blows from a heavy object. Carol Fisher had been shot in the hand and shot in the back as she tried to escape. She had staggered 60 feet down the garden path before she collapsed and was shot in the neck while on the ground. Blows to her head resulted in extensive fractures to the front of her skull which caused her death.

Mr William Boyce, QC, prosecuting, read out statements made by Robert Firkins to the police in which he said they had gone to Cornwall to buy puff (cannabis) and spend time with relatives. "Me and my brother have nothing to with this murder. I swear it on my baby's life, my life, everybody's life."

Lee Firkins had told the police, "I would not do a murder, or do a robbery on these people, or anything like that. It is sick, evil and ghastly. It was nothing to do with us. This is genuine, sincere and I mean it".

The prosecutor questioned Lee Firkins about the Fraddon robbery when he had carried a shotgun. "Were you going to fire it?", asked Mr Boyce. "If need be", replied the defendant. "If the person you are robbing is too slow to give you the money it would need to be fired?" "Oh yes", Lee Firkins said. Asked if he had ever fired a shotgun before 19 December Lee Firkins told the court, "Not to my knowledge, no".

Mr Boyce pointed out to the jury that the killers had had the "nous" to collect the spent shotgun cartridges from the Fishers' bungalow before leaving the scene. Those spent cartridges could have been used as evidence.

Mr Boyce presented to the jury the series of serious offences that the brothers had admitted committing soon after the murder of the Fishers. Mr Chawla, for the defence, told the jury that evidence of criminality for other offences was not evidence which proved their guilt in these murders. He said there was no scientific evidence to connect the defendants to the garage or the bungalow.

During his summing up Mr Justice Owen told the jury the evidence would have aroused "understandable" feelings of horror and revulsion for the "senseless and appallingly savage" killings. He instructed, "You must put all such feelings and emotions to one side and they must not be allowed to colour your judgement. Consider the evidence in a calm, dispassionate and critical manner".

When the jury foreman announced that they had unanimously found both defendants "Guilty", the brothers swore and shouted abuse from the dock. As Mr Justice Owen started to pronounce the sentence, he was interrupted by a shout of "We are two innocent men". The brothers were taken from the Court and the judge said, "You burst in on Mr and Mrs Fisher, a happy, close, self-contained couple and brutally extinguished their lives with extreme violence. Both were shot a number of times which would have been fatal had they not already been beaten with a sledgehammer". The judge said some measure of the "indescribable horror" that the brothers had inflicted was that as she attempted to dial 999, Mrs Fisher's hand was shot away, almost severing it. She was shot again in the back. She had almost made it to the garden gate when she was shot again, then clubbed to death with a sledgehammer. He said he would determine the minimum term the brothers must serve when he sentenced them for the other offences which the jury had heard admitted.

Mr Justice Owen sentenced each brother to life imprisonment. He said there were no mitigating circumstances and he ordered that they must spend 26 years in jail before being eligible to be considered for parole. The brothers were given leave to appeal.

The Court of Appeal ordered the Criminal Cases Review Commission, which investigates possible miscarriages of justice, to examine the evidence given by the cell-mate and his subsequent conduct. Another police force was ordered to look into the circumstances of evidence gathered from the cellmate and its reliability. In December 2009, a year and a half after the convictions, the Court of Appeal upheld them. The judges found that after the fullest investigation nothing had been uncovered to raise doubts about the truthfulness of the cellmate's evidence.

At the appeal the prisoner, who had given the critical evidence that enabled the police to put together a case, was referred to as "Witness X" because he had been taken into the Witness Protection Scheme. He was hoping to be eligible for the £10,000 reward. The rejection of the appeal brought closure for the Fishers' relatives, for the police and for the prosecution.

The boarded-up bungalow and Perch Garage were demolished in 2007. A new business and a new home were planned for the site.

CHAPTER 11

Mystery Remains: Unsolved Cases

S ome people have got away with murder, or so it would seem from the cases still open in Cornwall.

A brutal double murder was discovered at Skinners Bottom, about seven miles north-west of Truro, on 25 January 1920. Joseph Charles Hoare, a cattle dealer and farmer, aged 57, a bachelor, and Laura Sara, a married woman, aged 40, were found in the garden of their home with their heads severely battered. Dr Forsyth, a doctor practising in Chacewater, was sent for but Mr Hoare died five minutes after being found and Mrs Sara died two hours later. Neither regained consciousness.

When the bodies were found it appeared that Mr Hoare had been attacked and bludgeoned with a heavy piece of tree branch, and managed to get to the garden gate before falling where he was found. Mrs Sara had come out in bare feet and in her nightclothes to see what was happening and she too had been felled to the ground, just outside the front door.

There were no signs of a struggle in the house or of it having been ransacked. Mr Hoare kept cash on his person in a little cloth bag and large sums of cash in the house. The empty bag was found in his waistcoat pocket and the cash in the house was undisturbed. Mr Hoare and Mrs Sara had been living happily together for two years.

He was of a quiet and peaceable disposition. She was of a fiery temper and fond of drink. She had left her husband of twenty years and was assumed to be Mr Hoare's housekeeper. When the police searched the house they found a bed showing signs that two people had slept in it.

A few days before these deaths, the Commissioner of the Metropolitan Police had made a statement saying he believed county and other constabularies would get a good deal of help from Scotland Yard if they asked for assistance without delay. Accordingly, Scotland Yard was asked by the County Police at Bodmin for help and sent down Chief Inspector Heldon, who led the search for the murderer or murderers. The motive for the crime was thought to be robbery or perhaps jealousy but exhaustive enquiries proved fruitless. Mr Hoare and Mrs Sara had been drinking in the Red Lion Inn in Blackwater with a stranger, who was never identified, on the night before they died.

At the Coroner's Inquest on 12 February the Chief Inspector said the only feasible explanation was that the couple had killed one another. He said that Joseph Hoare had loved Laura Sara wholeheartedly but she only used the man to get possession of his smallholding and cash. The Chief Inspector revealed that Joseph Hoare had made a Will in favour of Laura Sara and that it was his belief that she was tired of Hoare, and country life, and determined to kill him in order to benefit from his estate. The Chief Inspector theorised that when Mr Hoare left the farmhouse that morning, Mrs Sara followed him, in bare feet, to the cowshed where she took the murder weapon from the pile of logs kept beside the building. Outside the cowshed she struck Joseph Hoare on the forehead causing fatal injuries. He had wrested the stick from her and hit her two or three times before he missed a blow and the wood fell from his hand. Hoare fell beside the cowshed but regained sufficient strength to walk to where he was found.

Dr Forsyth gave evidence that Joseph Hoare's frontal bone had been broken in five places by a blow which the woman was physically capable of inflicting. The Coroner asked if it would have been physically possible for the woman to have struck the blow after she herself had been injured. Dr Forsyth said "No. Nor could the man have inflicted the injuries on the woman after he had been injured". The doctor did not believe the man would have been able to stand up after he was struck nor would he have been able to throw the stick to the spot where it was found.

The Coroner summed up the evidence for the jury and said it came down to whether the detective was right, or the doctor. Seven of the eight jurymen found the doctor's evidence clear and emphatic and returned a verdict of "Wilful murder against some person or persons unknown".

❋ ❋ ❋

On 14 December 1953 a farmer, Norman Wills, aged 39, was found face down in a stream on his 220 acre farm, Lodge Barton, near Liskeard. Mr Wills was one of five brothers in a family that had suffered a number of suicides. Norman's father committed suicide; one brother hanged himself; another shot his daughter and then himself; and, later, another brother shot himself through the head with a .22 rifle.

On the morning of his death, Norman Wills followed his usual routine but failed to return to the farmhouse. A brother living in the house and another living nearby began a search for him. They were joined later by two forestry workers who found Mr Wills face down in a fourteen inch deep stream. Only one set of footprints led from the farm to the dead man so the family assumed Norman Wills had committed suicide. He was known to have been upset the previous day when he was fined in the Magistrates' Court for failing to keep up-to-date records. The Cornwall County Pathologist, Dr F D M Hocking, however, noticed that on the opposite bank of the stream there were plenty of footprints.

The brothers lifted Norman Wills from the stream and were to tell Dr Hocking that the body had not been caught up in any way and that they had not touched the neck.

The post-mortem found there was no water in the lungs, as there would have been had death been due to drowning. There were a number of bruises to the neck, a fracture of the hyoid bone, and the tongue was bruised. As these are all symptoms of manual strangulation, Dr Hocking reported that as the cause of death. Professor Webster, Home Office Pathologist in Birmingham, agreed with Dr Hocking but the police did not. Dr Hocking sought the opinion of the Professor of Forensic Pathology at Leeds University, Professor Polson, who agreed there were aspects of the case which favoured either suicide or murder, and his inclination was that the death had been suicide.

The Coroner, Dr E S Toogood, told the jury that originally all the evidence tended to show that Norman Wills was worried about the proceedings taken against him in the Magistrates' Court and it was thought he had died by his own hand. The post-mortem finding of manual strangulation showed the death to be murder, although there had been no suggestion of a reason why anyone would strangle Mr Wills. A verdict of "Manual strangulation not self-inflicted" was brought in by the jury.

❋ ❋ ❋

The fully clothed body of 34 year old Mrs Susan Russell was found on the beach at Mylor below the high-tide mark on 3 January 1976. She lived with her husband, William Russell, a financier, in a house near the beach at Mylor. They had moved to Mylor from Hertfordshire in an effort, at least on Mrs Russell's part, to save their marriage which had been damaged by Mr Russell's infidelity and particularly by an affair with a Mrs Diane Malden. The Cornwall County Pathologist, Dr F D M Hocking, examined the body and reported that Mrs Russell had not died from drowning. She had vomited at the time of her death and food almost completely filled her windpipe, blocking both passages to her lungs, which were dry. Damage to Mrs Russell's neck indicated manual strangulation. Dr Hocking pronounced death was due to manual strangulation and suffocation due to terminal inhalation of vomit.

Devon and Cornwall Constabularies had recently amalgamated and they appointed Home Office Pathologist, Dr Hunt, to perform an autopsy on their behalf, the result of which agreed with Dr Hocking's findings. The dead woman's husband employed Professor Cameron, Director of the Forensic Department of The London Hospital, to examine his wife's remains. He appeared to agree with the other pathologists. Professor Keith Mant of the Forensic Department of Guy's Hospital found manual strangulation to be the cause of death. He reported that the force of the injuries meant they could not have been self-inflicted. Apparently ignoring Dr Hocking's finding that there was no sea-water in the lungs, Professor Mant opined that Mrs Russell had been alive when she was thrown into the sea.

During the ten months that the forensic examinations were taking place, the police continued their search for someone who had manually strangled Mrs Russell. William Russell was an obvious suspect as it was well-known that the Russells did not get on together. On the night of Mrs Russell's death they had had a serious quarrel. She had thrown her wedding ring at her husband and stormed out. After she had gone, Mr Russell said he found £500 was missing. Mr Russell claimed not to have seen his wife alive after she left the house. He said that for several nights recently she had left home for about one hour and that he had no idea where she went. Police enquiries failed to find anyone who had seen Mrs Russell on the night of her death.

Ten months after Mrs Russell's death, her 35 year old husband was charged with her murder. He appeared before Penryn Magistrates' Court on 21 October 1976. Dr Hocking, Dr Hunt and Professor Mant gave evidence about the cause of Mrs Russell's death. Mr Graham Neville, for the defence, argued that all the evidence the prosecution had presented was circumstantial "and slender at that". Mr Neville said the Court's only conclusion could be that Mrs Russell, "a devoted mother and clinging wife" according to the prosecution, had been murdered but that there was no evidence to link the husband with the crime. The prosecution, he added, had failed to make out a *prima facie* case.

Penryn Magistrates found there was no case for Mr Russell to answer and discharged him. Four months later the District Coroner, Mr Carlyon, returned an open verdict and so the case has not been solved.

In February 1985, at a time when he was in deep financial trouble, William Russell's body was found on the ground below the window of his room in a hotel in Spain.

❊ ❊ ❊

Ruan High Lanes on the Roseland Peninsula would be a very quiet corner of Cornwall with light traffic if it were not for the fact that the road to and from the King Harry Ferry over the river Fal passes through it. On the afternoon of 20 October 1988, Lyn Bryant, a 40 year old married mother of two, set out to walk the family dog down the lanes around her home at Ruan High Lanes. An hour later she was found lying in the gateway to a field. Her throat had been cut and she had been stabbed five times in the neck, chest and back with a small-bladed knife. Extensive police enquiries found no witnesses and no motive. At one time the police investigated whether Lyn Bryant's murder was linked to the unsolved murder of a dog-walking schoolgirl, Kate Bushell, near Exeter, but despite some similar features they were unable to be certain there was a connection.

Four months after the discovery of Lyn Bryant's body, the gold and tortoiseshell spectacles she had been wearing, were found lying in the gateway where she had died. This raised the possibility that the murderer had returned to the scene of the crime but to date no-one has been arrested.

✳ ✳ ✳

On Sunday, 12 April 2002 the 71 year-old millionaire, Les Bate, was found by his son, Martin, lying in a pool of blood near the back door of his isolated, detached, home. At first it was thought death was the result of an accidental fall but the post-mortem revealed that Les Bate had been beaten about the head and body so badly that he had broken ribs and internal injuries.

Les Bate was a self-made multi-millionaire who owned four farms and a great deal of land. Stocky, 5'2" tall, Mr Bate was very proud of his achievements. Everyone in and around Chapel Amble knew him, with opinion of him varying from his daughter's, "He was a loveable rogue – a true Cornish character", to those who thought he "rubbed people up the wrong way" and was "cantankerous" and "flashy".

Chapel Amble, a hamlet about five miles from the north coast town of Rock, has about one hundred inhabitants, a village green, a few shops and a pub, The Maltsters Arms, well-known for its award-winning food and friendly atmosphere. It is said that there was no record of a violent crime being committed in Chapel Amble since 1373.

The police decided there was a "local angle" to the killing. Mr Bate had spent his last night in The Maltsters entertaining the regulars with colourful tales of a lifetime in farming and with his unrestrained views on politics. It was a Friday night and there were about thirty people in the pub; some eating in the restaurant, others drinking in the bar and the lounge. Mr Bate kept producing his tan leather folding wallet bulging with money, estimated to be £1,000, and the barman cautioned him not to show his money so openly. Mr Bate responded by producing a cheque for £11,000 and showing it to those at the bar. At 11.30pm Mr Bate got into his red Land Rover Discovery and drove two miles to his home. The police suspected that either someone followed him home and pounced on him as he went to enter the farmhouse through the back door or, familiar with his habits, waited in the darkness and attacked him as he unlocked the door.

A police team of fifty officers made house-to-house enquiries and finger-printed and DNA tested every worker or drinker who was at the pub that night. They searched fields and hedges for Les Bate's folding tan wallet and the £1,000 believed to be in it. The wallet, the cash and the cheque have never been found. Seven months earlier, Mr Bate's house had been broken into and £25,000 was taken together with jewellery, paintings and other valuables. No-one was charged with that offence but it was said to have made Mr Bate more security conscious.

The fact that the police are convinced there is a local angle to the killing has caused a climate of suspicion amongst the villagers but to date no-one has been arrested.

* * *

On the morning of 6 November 2004, Joan Roddam, a former hair-dresser, was seen alive at her isolated bungalow in the hamlet of West Downs, near Delabole, to which she and her husband had retired in 1982. The 74 year old widow had lived alone with three cats since the death of her husband in 1997. Two days later Joan Roddam was found dead in the back garden of her home, wearing only her nightclothes. The police quickly ruled out a connection between this murder and the brutal murder of Graham and Carol Fisher at Perch Garage, some fifteen miles away, on Guy Fawkes' Night. Mrs Roddam had been suffocated by her killer. There were no signs of forced entry at the bungalow and it had not been ransacked. The police believed Mrs Roddam knew her killer but could find no motive for the crime.

Bibliography

Bird, S., (2002). *Cornish Tales of Mystery and Murder.* Newbury: Countryside Books.

Department of Health and Social Security, (1978). *Report of the Social Work Service of the DHSS into certain aspects of the management of the case of Stephen Menheniott.* London: HMSO.

Hocking, F.D.M., (1992). *Bodies and Crimes. A Pathologist Speaks.* Brighton: Book Publishing Guild Ltd.

Hyde, H.M., (1964). *Norman Birkett: The Life of Lord Birkett of Ulverston.* London: Hamish Hamilton.

Purchas, J., (1986). *Death on the Isles of Scilly. The Grave in California Field.* Redruth: Dyllansow Truran.

The Times

Van der Kiste, J. and Sly, N., (2007). *Cornish Murders.* Stroud: The History Press Ltd.

Western Morning News

Williams, M., (1980). *Cornish Mysteries.* Launceston: Bossiney Books.

Wilson, C. (ed.), (1975). *Murder in the Westcountry.* Launceston: Bossiney Books.